RACE Method Boot Camp — Book Two

Equipping Anti-Racism Allies: Unitarian Universalist Edition

By David W. Campt PhD

@thedialogueguy

www.whiteallytoolkit.com

with Allison Mahaley

www.myredfern.com

I AM Publications

Equipping Anti-Racism Allies: Unitarian Universalist Edition
RACE Method Boot Camp — Book Two
Copyright © 2020 by David W. Campt with Allison Mahaley

I AM Publications
(617) 564-1060
contact@iampubs.com
www.iampubs.com

First Edition, 2020

ISBN: 978-1-943382-06-4

Foreword

On November 9th, 2016, I had a sermon to rewrite. I had five days to not only make sense of the 2016 election, but find a way to help my own UU Congregation in rural North Carolina make sense of it. I knew there would be a lot of new faces there that morning, also looking for some sort of a guarantee that not everyone had fallen for the ruse. What I landed on was what I know. I know Midwesterners. I know the loss they have experienced, the frustration they have, and the all-out fear in their hearts as their way of life has seriously shifted in the last generation from family farms to corporate models run by foreign entities. As the minister, it was my goal to help my congregation connect the dots and not only make sense of the election, but decide how we, as people of faith, would respond.

It sounds pretty simple. We are a denomination that prides itself on being the most educated of all progressive religions. We are the big tent religion. We take everyone: Buddhists, Muslims, Catholics, Pagans, Presbyterians, Humanists, the un-churched — our doors are wide open. So, we love diversity of spirit, but the truth is, our church is white; in fact, most UU churches are predominately white. Though we claim to be liberal, and know historically we fought for civil rights, we failed along with most other progressive churches to effectively confront our race issue. So, as the spiritual leader of the congregation, I began searching for resources to offer not just my congregants, but my entire community.

It is not easy to untangle the needs of such a theologically diverse group of well-intended people who span multiple generations. Even before the election, we had stumbled through frustrating conversations between young and old about whether Black Lives Matter was a good slogan for the movement. Most of our members had an affinity for Reverend William Barber and supported the Poor People's Campaign, but even Moral Monday supporters felt like "there were too many issues for just one sign." Intersectionality is a hard concept if you don't have a deep understanding of critical race theory, so is it necessary for everyone to have that depth of understanding before we make a difference?

After about a year of casting about for resources, we finally settled on a curriculum that was just the right amount of historical context, critical race theory, and call to action to fit my community. We ran through it the first time and realized, while the theories and underpinnings were excellent, it was still lacking skill-based techniques to actually empower people to make a difference. Luckily, that was right around the time we met Dr. Campt.

The White Ally Toolkit was the perfect fit for us. The skills of compassionate listening are the foundational building blocks of our covenantal faith — where the rubber meets the road of siding with love when we engage with others. Increasing our capacity for compassionate listening not only promises to move the needle on ending racism in our community, it will make our community healthier and more resilient. It will deepen our relationships as we live out our values of liberal religious theology. We have the power to make the world a better place, we just need the skills to do it. I am so happy that Dr. Campt (and my congregant Allison Mahaley have adapted his Boot Camp to include spiritual practices for grounding, calming, and focusing on the positive impact individuals can have on the world. At our best, we can be the change agents this world so desperately needs.

Welcome to the journey,
Patty

Rev. Patty Hanneman
Minister of Unitarian Universalist Congregation of Hillsborough
Community Partnering Congregation for the Love Resists Campaign

Preface

As you will see, liberal religious principles and Unitarian Universalists core values are embodied in the approach laid out in the readings and activities of each of the 30 steps of this Boot Camp. These universal ideals will be important for us to call upon as we aim towards our goals: a beloved community built on radical inclusion, an acknowledgment of our interdependence, much deeper acceptance across societal divides, and our own more consistent commitment to spiritual growth.

Inevitably, moving toward these goals will mean we must try to create a community where everyday interactions are rooted in a stance of love and a habit of deep listening. If we see it as our personal responsibility to be forces of love and of deep compassion, we become part of the solution.

The major attitudinal shift involved in the RACE Method approach to racial equity work is that we must seek a higher level of acceptance of people whom we think of as having an undeveloped, problematic or perhaps troubling way of thinking about race and racism. We must find a different way of thinking about the distinction between the people we will work on (whom we must accept) and their views on racism (which we are trying to change).

The notion of radical acceptance may provide a useful way of discussing the values we aspire to. In radical acceptance, we are not fighting with current realities in the world - or within us, for that matter - but rather we are deeply accepting what is true now and holding hope for what might be. From that place of acceptance, we are making choices about what we want to do in order to create what might be.

How this Partnership Came to Be

The partnership between David and Allison was born in early 2019 when David began focusing on the potential of North Carolina audiences. As the recipient of the Unitarian Universalist Service Committee's Love Resists grant for grassroots organizing, Allison has been working explicitly to bring along white allies for over 4 years. Both an employee of a UU congregation and a member of a separate UU congregation, she has been deeply enmeshed in the UU world. While she has been offering workshops on racial construct theory and white privilege – especially white people's need for safety resulting in the over-policing of black and brown people - she was often left feeling like her audiences were mentally ready, but ill-equipped to engage in making change. Simply understanding covenantal relationships and possessing a commitment to community, unfortunately, was not enough and seemed to leave most white people feeling inadequate to tackle racism.

The skills focus of the ACT Initiative was very attractive to Allison. She was overjoyed to learn the RACE method – which is a compassionate listening-based strategy of influencing people about racism – and quickly began thinking about ways this method might expand her anti-racism organizing. For his part, meeting Allison seemed like a blessing to David, since he had recognized that very important spiritual work is at the core of the project, but he had not yet put this idea at the leading edge of the project since he had been interacting with a wide variety of potential collaborators.

David and Allison very quickly recognized that a collaboration might be mutually beneficial in a number of ways. The two began working together closely and talking almost daily. The idea of revising the original Boot Camp as a spiritual journey, including rituals for self-reflection and relaxation grounded in UU values, was born out of pure mutual enthusiasm. Allison and David are proud to offer this workbook to people of faith who believe that every spiritual journey involves both personal and communal transformation.

How Does this Book Relate to the Movement Towards an 8Th UU Principle on Dismantling Racism?

Within the UU community, there is a growing movement to adopt an 8th principle focused on racial equity. The principle is stated as follows:

> *"We, the member congregations of the Unitarian Universalist Association, covenant to affirm and promote: journeying toward spiritual wholeness by working to build a diverse multicultural Beloved Community by our actions that accountably dismantle racism and other oppressions in ourselves and our institutions."*

This workbook is offered in full recognition of the way that racism undermines individuals' spiritual development, the UU community's progress, and the health of the United States and all nations. In this workbook, we have not highlighted this 8th principle explicitly - partially because the adoption of this principle is still in progress, and partially because this principle is the driving force of the entire book.

We think of ourselves as people whose careers have largely been devoted to the cause of dismantling racism. Thus, our hope is that this Boot Camp adds more weight to the growing recognition within the UU community of the centrality of engaging with racism as a core spiritual challenge. We cannot experience the full blossoming of our humanity if we do not grapple with the often sometimes subtle and sometimes obvious ways that racism undermines our collective present and common future.

Namaste and blessed be.

Spiritual Touchstones of this Edition

This edition of the RACE Method Boot Camp represents an effort to more explicitly surface the spiritual dimensions of this work, and of all the products of this initiative. Furthermore, this edition expressly refers to twelve important ideas, delineated below, which are the 7 Core Principles of Unitarian Universalists and the Five Smooth Stones of Religious Liberalism. The principles are accepted as the uniting ideas of the Unitarian Universalism. The Five Smooth Stones were originally popularized in a 1976 work by James Luther Adams called "Guiding Principles for a Free Faith" in *On Being Human Religiously: Selected Essays in Religion and Society*, Max Stackhouse, ed. Beacon Press, 1976, pp. 12-20.

Seven Principles of Unitarian Universalism

1st Principle: The inherent worth and dignity of every person;

2nd Principle: Justice, equity and compassion in human relations;

3rd Principle: Acceptance of one another and encouragement to spiritual growth in our congregations;

4th Principle: A free and responsible search for truth and meaning;

5th Principle: The right of conscience and the use of the democratic process within our congregations and in society at large;

6th Principle: The goal of world community with peace, liberty, and justice for all;

7th Principle: Respect for the interdependent web of all existence of which we are a part.

Five Smooth Stones of Religious Liberalism

Stone 1: "Religious liberalism depends on the principle that 'revelation' is continuous." Our religious tradition is a living tradition because we are always learning new truths.

Stone 2: "All relations between persons ought ideally to rest on mutual, free consent and not on coercion." We freely choose to enter into relationships with one another.

Stone 3: "Religious liberalism affirms the moral obligation to direct one's effort toward the establishment of a just and loving community. It is this which makes the role of the prophet central and indispensable in liberalism." Justice.

Stone 4: "...[W]e deny the immaculate conception of virtue and affirm the necessity of social incarnation." Agency: Good things don't just happen; people make them happen.

Stone 5: "[L]iberalism holds that the resources (divine and human) that are available for the achievement of meaningful change justify an attitude of ultimate optimism." Hope.

Introduction

Congratulations for deciding to engage in the Ally Conversation Toolkit's RACE Method Boot Camp. By engaging in the content of this journal, you are embarking on a journey that has the potential to positively affect your relationships over the course of your entire lifetime. What's more, your participation will enhance your ability to address one of the United States' and the world's most pressing problems—racism.

Kudos to you for your efforts to make the world a better place.

This Boot Camp will guide you in taking some important steps on your way to becoming a Compassionate Warrior for reducing racial hierarchies and divisions. The Ally Conversation Toolkit (ACT) often uses the term Compassionate Warrior for a few reasons. First, the struggle against racism is a multi-front war, which has us squaring off against the baser instincts of human nature, against our societal conventions about how groups relate to each other, and against structures and systems that continue to reinforce that some groups of people are innately more deserving than others. Many people who are on this journey have been committed to this process for years and know that this struggle has the complexity and breadth of a war.

But unlike many wars where the goal is to defeat "the enemy," the Compassionate Warrior takes the position that the best way to win the war against racism is to focus on compassion for those who appear to be on the other side, potentially to shine a light that is transformative for those in the dark. From this perspective, the war is largely about freeing people from a blindness that is engulfing them; in other words, the goal is to reveal the ways in which societal racism functions to blind a large number of people to its existence.[1]

> The ACT Initiative aims to significantly reduce the percentage of white Americans who think that racism against white people is just as important a social problem as racism against people of color— 55 % in 2017. The goal of the initiative is to catalyze a cultural shift so that this figure is reduced to 45% by 2025.

How does this blindness happen? People are persuaded that racial hierarchies in society and in their own perceptions are natural, or perhaps even what higher powers have ordained. If one has accepted this mindset, the people at the lower ends of the racial hierarchy become less deserving of compassion, respect, and even material resources.

Many anti-racism advocates find it hard to extend compassion to people who have racist views or who tend to deny racism's existence. It is a natural response to deny compassion to those who deny it to others; the desire to "return fire" lies deep in the human heart. It turns out, though, that this response is not helpful to the problem of subverting people's racism. There is ample evidence from many fields of science that the best way to enhance the compassion of people who lack it is to show compassion to those people. To quote Dr. Martin Luther King, Jr., "Only light can drive out darkness."

The RACE Method Boot Camp, as well as the other elements of the ACT Initiative, is for people who, in the war to dismantle racism, aspire to be warriors who are willing to make compassion both their goal and their prime weapon.

---

1   Compassionate Warriors are focused on healing that blindness.

Since the Fall 2018 original publication of the RACE Method Boot Camp — Book One, it has become increasingly clear that the original edition under-emphasized the spiritual underpinnings of this Ally Conversation Toolkit initiative. As people have engaged with this material, it has become more clear to the ACT team that the decision to engage deeply held interpersonal differences from a stance of compassion is an act of heart and mind that requires a rather profound rearrangement of one's internal mechanisms and habits. This spiritual edition of the Boot Camp represents recognition of how difficult this work is. As such, it attempts to provide additional material to support this deeply spiritual transformative journey.

Premises of this Initiative

- Today, about 55% of white people believe that racism against whites is just as important a societal problem as racism against people of color. The fact that so many whites hold this view is a problem that undermines America.
- Though they may be more difficult to execute, strategies for influencing people based on compassion and empathy are likely to work better than those based on verbal combat, shaming, or other verbally aggressive methods.
- It is important for anti-racism allies to develop their own understanding of societal racism and awareness of how whiteness and other racial realities function.
- However, doing this internal work should NOT be thought of as a necessary precursor to the work of effectively engaging others who don't think that racism against people of color is real and a problem worth addressing.
- Put directly: People who think racism is problem should immediately start trying to influence others, even without additional reading, support groups, and training.

According to Tricia De Beer of Greensboro, North Carolina, an adult education specialist who, along with her husband John, created a multi-month group engagement process around the Boot Camp, "It is critical to tell people that this is very hard work. If you engage this material," she said, "you will be changing the norms of your relationships with others, and your habits of how you think you should relate to others. This is deep emotional and spiritual work." With that in mind, we offer this new edition.

The natural reaction most people have to ideas they find repugnant or merely distasteful – or to the people who have these ideas – is to: 1) defeat them (fight), 2) minimize our exposure (flight), or 3) hope that the distasteful entity has not noticed us (freeze). All these reactions lead to polarization and isolation is our communities and society at large. Particularly in modern western cultures that emphasize either conflict or emotional safety, it is not natural to pursue a fourth reaction that is unlike the three above. The primary habit this effort seeks is to embrace moments when differences emerge as opportunities to do some useful work — on them, on yourself, and most likely both.

The RACE Method that this initiative promotes is about rearranging many things — our self-conception, our habits, our relationships, and hopefully, our society.

Important Premises and Cautions

There are a few premises of this initiative that are listed in th sidebar. It is useful to review these premises before you go too much further with this document. Although you may not wholeheartedly agree with every one of them, having deep misgivings with some of them may inhibit you from benefiting from the processes suggested in this workbook.

Unless you believe the premises more than you question them, the process of engaging these methods here may lead to more frustration or confusion than clarity and useful guidance. If you are basically on board with these ideas, there are two additional points that are worth noting and remembering.

First, just as in the military, a Boot Camp is merely an intensive, initial training experience that prepares warriors to simply begin learning the necessary skills to master tasks that lie ahead of them. Learning to become effective at engaging people who are skeptical about racism is a lifelong process; this is only an initial booster shot to that journey.

Moreover, the journey toward becoming a Compassionate Warrior against racism is one that has many dimensions. The focus of this journal is on one particular task—engaging in one-on-one and very small group conversations with people who question the idea that racism against people of color is a specific national problem worth special attention. It is vital that large numbers of people have more such conversations successfully with racism skeptics as a vital part of the anti-racism movement. Engaging in these difficult conversations is an activity that is often not sufficiently emphasized by the denizens of the movement.

Nevertheless, please remember that engaging people who deny or minimize racism is not the only important task for anti-racism allies. Others include working on one's self-awareness, improving one's interactions with people of color, appropriately collaborating within liberation movements, and building an interracial beloved community, among many others. So even if you dramatically improve your effectiveness, you should not declare yourself sufficiently "woke" and no longer in need of any additional self-improvement. As long as systemic racism still exists, none of us need to be overly confident that we are doing as much as we can to dismantle it.

Why Highlight Ideas from Unitarian Universalism?

As this project devotes more explicit attention to the spiritual dimensions of adopting the RACE Method to dismantle racism, the second edition of this document explicitly draws connections between the daily tasks of improving allyship to the 7 Principles of UUism. Unitarian Universalists have embodied the imperfectly pursued struggle to dismantle white supremacy and to create the enormous cultural shift required to not only go beyond lip service to the notion of equality, but also to transfer actual power to people of color in their organization and make room for them to lead. It is bruising work in which mistakes are inevitable…and UUs have made many.

But the covenantal relationships that require a calling back rather than a casting out provide enough of a safety net to persevere. The UU aspiration of calling back rather than splitting apart arguably sets UUs apart from Christianity and some other faith traditions. UU is the big tent church where any person of faith and hope can seek a spiritual home. But the 7 Principles (an 8th one is being discerned) do not go far enough to ready the ground for transformational work. As a result, we added to the 7 Principles of Unitarian Universalism an additional resource that is widely appreciated by UUs and some others: Five Smooth Stones of Religious Liberalism.

So, why these specific ideas that emerge from a specific tradition?

First, Unitarian congregations have been the group that has most frequently and enthusiastically resonated with the mission of the ACT initiative. This project has collaborated with a wide variety of organizations including Chambers of Commerce, conflict resolution programs, civil rights and activist groups, and a wide variety of faith groups. The pursuit of such collaborations will continue, since the goal of this project is to catalyze a very large-scale change in the ways that white people think about racism.

At the same time, it is clear that a disproportionate number of these partnerships have happened with Unitarian Universalist Fellowships and Congregations. There appears to be a particularly high level of natural resonance between the compassion-based strategy of dismantling racism used in this project and the culture of Unitarian Universalism. Since this is the case, it seems sensible to start here.

Over time, this project aspires to produce other customized versions of the Boot Camp. It is not hard to imagine a future that has inspirational content specifically for Buddhists, Jews, subsets of Christians, and other faith traditions. (In fact, the project would welcome being contacted by people who want to partner to create such materials.) For the moment, given what appears to be the natural synergies between the project and Unitarian Universalists, this seems a good place to launch an initial effort to customize these materials.

In addition, Unitarian Universalism is intentionally positioned to welcome people from a variety of faiths, as well as the many who identify as spiritual but not religious. As a result, the spiritual ideas that will contextualize the daily actions in this Boot Camp build upon ideas that are likely to have resonance with people from a variety of perspectives. Conceivably, the 12 spiritual ideas that flavor this document should provide nourishment for non-Unitarians, in addition to having deep resonance within the Unitarian Universalist community, because the ideas are commonly talked in those congregations.

About the RACE Method

People do not like the feeling that you are running a program on them. Your goal is to become facile enough with the process so that it feels natural and not stilted.

Often, people will respond with queries about why they believe what they believe with "facts" they have heard from the media. Sometimes, you will have to give them extra encouragement to get them to focus the conversation on their actual lived experiences. This might look like: "I bet those facts wouldn't ring true if you did not have an experience that confirmed them. That is what I really want to hear about." Or, "I trust people's experiences much better than media reports, since there is so much bad media out there. I want to know what you have personally seen about this."

There are people whose views about race are so entrenched or their conversational style is so toxic that it does not make sense to engage them. As Dr. Eddie Moore (pictured, right)" of the White Privilege Conference says, "There are some pancakes that cannot be flipped." While Compassionate Warriors are bold and open to difficult tasks, they also recognize that it is important to not waste energy on people who are beyond reach.

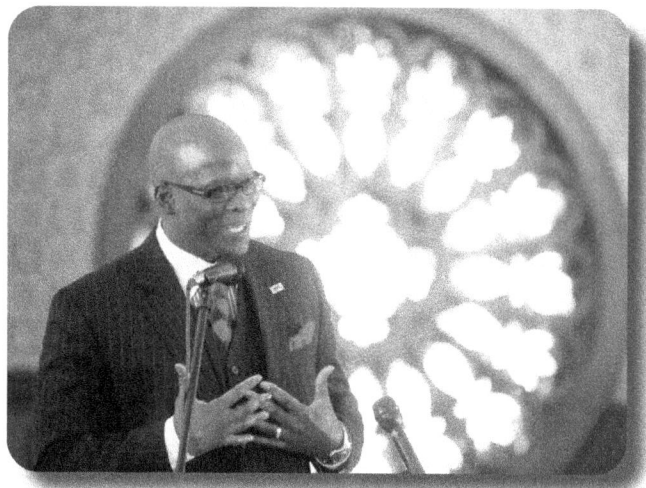

The RACE Method Boot Camp is based on the finding that conversational approaches using respectful dialogue, empathy, and story telling are more effective in influencing people compared with conversational styles that emphasize factual information, debate, combat, and shaming people.

A critical task for influencing people is to remain calm and centered, and not emotionally activated when disagreement on the issues occurs. It is valuable to have pre-rehearsed strategies that you can use to calm yourself if necessary. It is also helpful to have self-management strategies that you can invoke during the conversation to help you regain a centered and calm place if you begin to stray.

One primary reason that factual information does not work well when trying to persuade people around deeply held beliefs is due to something called the Backfire Effect. This psychological dynamic occurs is when people are confronted with facts that contradict deeply held beliefs, the tendency for the vast majority of people (from all ideological perspectives) is simply to discard the facts as "fake news" and recommit themselves to their beliefs. When people feel that someone is challenging deeply held beliefs, the part of the brain that is activated is the same part that is engaged when people perceive physical threats.

A key strategy in getting people to re-visit their points of view is to first establish a sense of rapport with them and get them to see you as someone who is like them, not someone in an opposing group. With its multiple offerings, the Ally Conversation Toolkit initiative is designed to help white allies have better conversations with racism skeptics in a wide variety of circumstances. For example, if you read the full 280 pages of the White Ally Toolkit Workbook, you will have reviewed specific material relevant to conversations about race and police, the belief that people of color are lazy, the idea that racial oppression was too long ago to talk about, and a host of other topics.

This Boot Camp is less comprehensive on the number of specific racially problematic statements it prepares you to address. Our goal here is to introduce the basic sensibility and methods of the initiative as well as give you some usable tools to navigate the most foundational topics in the disconnection between allies and skeptics. These foundational topics have to do with whether bias must be intentional to be problematic, whether there are advantages to being white, whether there has been significant racial progress that needs to be labeled as such, and whether explicit bigotry should be thought about differently than casual racial prejudice. These topics will be at the center of your Connect and Expand stories.

This Boot Camp will give you encouragement to develop your own personal stories about unconscious bias and about racial progress. The hope is that by the time the Boot Camp is over, you will have in your toolkit at least two pithy and compelling stories about the way that even you sometimes have racially biased thoughts. In addition, the aspiration is that by the end of the Boot Camp, you will have two pithy and compelling stories that explain why you believe that there has been some notable racial progress over recent decades. When interacting with racism skeptics, your racial progress and unconscious bias stories will serve as Connect and Expand stories, respectively.

About a third of the way through this experience, you will begin to focus on remembering, constructing, and delivering these stories. Before then, you will be working on vital skills — relaxing, asking questions, and listening — that you will need in order to deploy these stories effectively. Still, it is useful to make you aware of the topics of those stories, so that your unconscious and semi-conscious mind can begin probing your memory for experiences that will become the basis of the personal anecdotes in your toolkit.

Note to Group Leaders — The RACE Method Boot Camp is designed for individuals to use as a personal journey toward more effective allyship. The curriculum is easily adaptable for small groups or even religious education classes of any size. Instructions for adaptations are contained in the Appendices. The curriculum contains appropriate content for teens and young adults, though they may need more or less back-loading of critical race theory depending on their prior exposure to anti-racism information. Ideally, if teens are going to engage in the materials, it would be helpful for them be part of a multi-age group.

How this Boot Camp Can Be Used

By engaging the content of these materials, our hope is that you see the transformational power of anti-racism work as spirit lifting. Learning these centering and relaxation techniques along with approaches to dialogue will positively impact all your relationships. By intentionally linking values-based tenets to each step's exercises, you have the opportunity to deepen your understanding of the foundations of progressive liberal faith, and you will become empowered to bring your values into the world as an agent for positive change.

Undoubtedly, there are many ways of using the core content of this book, which is delineated into the 30 sequenced sets of daily instructions that will help a person achieve some initial facility in the core methods of the ACT initiative. Before reviewing three ways to use this document, here is a quick review of

how each Boot Camp step is presented:
- **Opening Words:** An opening quotation for motivation and contemplation that is relevant to the step's activities.
- **Grounding:** The articulation of one of the 7 Unitarian Principles and/or one of the Five Smooth Stones of Liberal Religion that seems most applicable.
- A brief comment, usually one to three paragraphs, that draws the connection between the Grounding and the step's tasks.
- **Goal:** The activities that will put you one step closer to creating more successful conversations about racism.
- **Doing:** Description of the step's tasks. The tasks are designed so that most people can complete them in less than 25 minutes. On most steps, a Reflection task included in the Doing description.
- **Closing Words:** An additional inspirational quote designed to capture the spirit of the task for each step.

Three Ways of Using this Document

1. As a Personal Guide for Integrating Improved Allyship with Spirituality

Even if you don't have a strong spiritual orientation, this edition of the Boot Camp can be useful to you, since it provides a purposefully sequenced series of quick tasks that an individual can do in order to incrementally become more skilled in engaging conversations about racism. If you have a spiritual orientation, the framing of each step's task in light of one's spiritual ideas will likely provide additional encouragement to the task of re-orienting how you engage difficult conversations. The hope is that the additional framing will ease the challenging process of revisiting many daily decisions, including whom we decide to talk to, how we engage people, what news sources we consume, and how we approach centering ourselves when conversations become stressful.

2. As an Aid to a Regular, Personal Ritual that Connects Allyship to Spiritual Growth

The infrmation in this document has been intentionally formatted to support people who might want to use it as a focused daily meditation. Some people might want this to be largely a mental meditation, while others might want to use this content as a regular spiritual ritual. Here is an example of the steps in a routine that someone might construct if they wanted to relate to the material in this way:
- Go to a calm and quiet place. Light a candle/chalice.
- Read the opening quotation; reflect on it.
- Read the grounding Principle/Smooth Stone for the step and then reflect on the link between this idea and the daily task. Do some contemplation of the applicability of these ideas to your life generally, and to the activities of the step.
- Read the daily task description and think about the way that engaging the task will be challenging but likely useful for your spiritual growth.
- Read the closing quote.
- Extinguish the candle/chalice.

On the vast majority of steps, you are encouraged to come back to the Boot Camp and write a short reflection on how the activity went. This also might be a time to reread the opening and/or closing quotation.

3. As the Basis of Group Study and/or a Group Ritual

The founders and promoters of this project have been overjoyed to learn that all across the United States, there are groups of people who are gathering in learning communities to support each other as they attempt to engage the methods discussed herein. The project team has been deeply gratified that this work has been engaged without the guidance of a leaders guide from the project!

People are more likely to be successful in learning new ways of relating to racism skeptics if they have regular conversations with other allies trying to train themselves in being more compassionate. Engaging in a group ritual with others about the connection between anti-racism allyship and spiritual goals could be very powerful. Arguably though, the greater value of the group experience is to provide a setting where people can share and compare, as well as challenge and support their efforts to reshape their response to others who see the world very differently. People need ongoing encouragement, and reinforcement that they are not the only ones who might be struggling. They also need to be buoyed by hearing about successes by others. Groups help on all these fronts.

To support learning groups, this edition includes a Leaders Guide Appendix that provides some suggestions for leaders who intend to use the Boot Camp in the context of group learning. The appendix includes factors to consider in setting up a group as well as agenda and exercises. Group leaders should recognize that in the rest of the document before the appendix, the tone reflects a presumption that the reader is engaging the document in a self-directed manner.

Context and Rationales for this Approach to Dismantling Racism

As noted above, the ACT initiative takes the position that large-scale efforts to dismantle systems racism in the United States will have limited success as long as majorities of the white population think that racism against people of color is not a specific problem meriting specific attention. Furthermore, an important strategy for moving public opinion is the large-scale engagement of person-to-person conversations in informal unfacilitated settings (such as the holiday dinner table) between the 45% of white people who think that racism against POCs merits specific attention (anti-racism allies) and the 55% who do not (racism skeptics).

How Should Anti-Racism Allies Conduct Themselves in These Conversations?

There is a school of thought within the ranks of many progressives that it is important to always counter racially problematic statements with aggressive counterattacks, rebuttals, denunciations, and similar tactics or total avoidance. According to this thinking, strategies based on listening, mobilizing compassion, and marshaling empathy only serve to coddle what is sometimes called white supremacy culture. According to this way of thinking, the decision by a white ally to adopt conversational strategies that are designed to lower defensiveness of a skeptic should be thought of as making a concession to white fragility.

Boot Camp Key Facts

- In the testing phase of these exercises 70% of the people completed the tasks in less than 25 minutes per step, and 55% in less than 20 minutes per step.
- For most steps, the bulk of your time will be spent on doing the exercise, not on reading. There are a few exceptions. Step 1 introduces you to the sensibilities and approach of the initiative, and has the most reading of any step. Steps 4, 7, 13, and 28 have less reading than step 1, but more than most steps. For the most part, the reading level is very light.
- Once every seven or eight steps, the task will focus on not talking to people, but rather will focus on making mental and written reflections of your recent progress.
- Some of the activities are not explicitly directed to issues related to race, but will help you get ready to have encounters that are race related.
- Each step includes "Expected" activities that should take no more than 20 minutes. On a few steps, there are "Bonus" activities that might take up to an additional 20 minutes.
- Increasing your ability to act from a place of empathy and compassion on racial issues is highly likely to help your interactions with people that concern other topics.

Equipping Anti-Racism Allies: UU Edition

While this is not an unreasonable perspective, the ACT has a different view. When you generate triggered behavior from someone, the compassionate response is to make strong effort to avoid further triggering them. Remember, white fragility is a symptom of undeveloped thinking and processing about racism. So, we may seem to lose battles by not directly and strongly confronting problematic behavior, but we are actually winning the war; in this case, by being a force that helps them move beyond white fragility, at least in the long run.

This project comes from the *opposite* view point to aggressive confrontation being the best way to move people away from racially problematic views. This initiative believes it is incumbent on allies — especially those who are white — to do the difficult work of training themselves to use approaches for challenging racism in one-on-one conversations using compassion-based methods. The reasoning is based on two major ideas:

1. There is strong evidence that empathy and compassion-based methods are more effective in persuading people.
2. Learning to use these strategies requires difficult emotional and spiritual work, and it is white folks who are best suited for doing this work. Below, each of these major ideas will be supported with be several additional points.

Empathy-Based Methods Work Better

People fighting racism should try to avoid the Backfire Effect: Facts Don't Matter

Over the past decade cognitive scientists have discussed the finding that introducing people to new facts or concepts is usually not effective for persuasion. Facts are particularly ineffective in trying to persuade people from positions that are deeply meaningful to them. Scientists who study cognition have found that when presented with facts that tend to contradict deeply held beliefs, the most common response is that people simply deepen their commitment to their belief, thus the term Backfire Effect.

The popularization of the term "fake news" provides a shorthand for how people tend to regard information presented as fact that tends to contradict deeply held beliefs. It is important to note that scientists have not noticed a discernible difference between ideological liberals and conservatives in their likelihood of being affected by the Backfire Effect.

Bottom line: When trying to persuade someone, don't focus on facts that contradict their perspective.

Being Listened to Empathetically Helps People Listen to Others with More Empathy.

During the past few years, scientists who study empathy have made a discovery that was considered unexpected. Specifically, social psychologists were examining the conditions under which Israeli Arabs engaged in an empathetic response to stories of Palestinian- Arab suffering. The scientists discovered that one powerful way the researchers could increase the empathetic response to stories of Palestinian suffering was to make sure that the Israeli Arabs had a chance to tell stories of their own suffering first.

Bottom line: When trying to persuade someone to increase their empathy toward someone, listen to their stories first.

Mirror Neurons and the Power of Stories

In the last several decades, brain scientists have concluded that there is a cognitive function that is often engaged that involves one person's brain state emulating what they perceive to be the brain state of another person whom they feel identified with in the moment. Most people have seen this in action when tears, laughter, or yawning becomes contagious and spreads to people who are not initially sad, mirthful, or sleepy. Brain researchers often use the term "mirror neurons" to describe the part of the brain that gets activated to create this replication effect in one person's brain from what is happening in another person's brain.

While the strength of mirror neurons varies substantially between people, the way to best to maximize this effect is to interact in ways that build rapport with the other person so that they identify with you. Demonstrating that you like them and consider yourself part of the same group are both strategies that can help you build rapport and connection with someone you are talking to. In addition, one of the best ways of doing that is to tell them a compelling story with you at the center of the story. Studies of brain scans of storytellers and listeners show that in cases when listeners report a story to be compelling, the listeners' brains light up in the same region as the storytellers'.

Bottom line: By honing our stories and telling them to others, we increase the chances that they will understand why we see things like we do.

Use the Reciprocity Principal to Your Advantage

Behavioral psychologists have noticed that humans and many other mammals have evolved a consistent pattern of behavior that involves individuals reciprocating beneficial actions that other members of their group have made. This is the part of us that feels obliged to put someone on our holiday card list if we receive one from someone or to invite people to our celebrations if someone invites us to theirs.

Bottom Line: If we ask someone to tell us a story and listen to them, most people will feel compunction to listen to our story.

All this together tells us that in order to persuade people around difficult topics like racism it is important that we:

- Become calm and centered when someone says something racist or denies racism exists.
- Avoid countering the person's beliefs with what you think of as facts.
- Ask questions to hear stories related to this belief and listen empathetically so that the person feels heard.
- Use rapport-building strategies, even though the person might have said something disturbing.
- Develop and tell stories that are experienced by the other person as relevant to the topic at hand.

Note: this sequence of task is the heart of the RACE method, which is the core strategy of this initiative. This will be explained in the reading on step 1.

For a person who feels strongly anti-racist, training oneself to reliably perform all these tasks in the face of racially problematic statement is difficult. Responding from a place of empathy and compassion to statements and people we perceive as part of the problem of systemic racism requires retraining ourselves — transcending, if you will, our initial reactions. Doing so is a spiritual task, if for no other reason than because it requires an emphasis on personal qualities that are spiritual, such as patience, empathy, discipline, and a deep conviction to see the goodness in people beyond their current behavior.

Every person could benefit from engaging in a personal practice to embed and hone compassionate listening skills. This initiative is based on the idea that it is particularly important for white anti-racism allies to engage these activities for the purpose of fighting racism.

To say it succinctly, the ACT initiative comes from the position that engaging racism skeptics in one-on-one conversation should be primarily white folks' work. Further, society should not rely on people of color to consistently engage these compassion-based strategies for interpersonal persuasion.

Why Dismantling Racism One Conversation at a Time Should Be White Folks' Work

Racism skeptics view people of color as less credible than white allies.

Though it may be uncomfortable to directly admit, many racism skeptics view POCs with less credibility in discussions about racism than fellow white people. Some of aspects of the reasoning behind this might be considered legitimate, while other asects of this reflect simple racism.

Legitimate Reason: During a conversation about whether racism against POCs is a national problem that impedes societal improvement, a racism skeptic might be inclined to perceive the perspective of a person of color with some additional incredulity because of reasonable assessments of the self-interest of the POC. If there is a greater societal recognition that racism is a problem, a person of color stands to potentially benefit from whatever remedies are created. Thus, it is not completely unreasonable or necessarily problematic for someone to view the POC in such a conversation as at least partially driven by self-interest.

Illegitimate Reason: At the same time, there is ample evidence that people of color are regarded through a lens that is racist and are viewed as less credible for this reason, which is clearly illegitimate factually, morally, and in other ways. For instance, as recently as 2015, 38 % of whites were willing to tell an anonymous surveyor than blacks are "less evolved" than whites. In 2016, 32% of whites reported that blacks were less industrious (i.e., lazier) than whites. These statistics only represent the estimated prevalence of consciously held views and do not include unconsciously held perspectives.[2]

Lowered impact of racial anxiety

The term racial anxiety refers to the increased nervousness that occurs in a cross- racial conversation when issues of race come up; the anxiety refers to concern about being perceived through a racialized lens. For white people, this anxiety appears in the form of worry about whether their statements/actions will be perceived as racist.

Racial anxiety has been demonstrated to have measurable physiological effects, such as the secretion of stress hormones that appear in saliva. It has been shown to be contagious and cause negative feedback loops, in that the increase in racial anxiety in one person can cause anxiety in the other person who was not initially affected by it.

Racial anxiety makes it much more difficult for people to be centered, rational, and to non-defensively evaluate ideas that challenge their thinking. While the increased polarization in the United States between conservatives and progressives probably has some implications for racial anxiety in cross-ideological encounters, there is established scientific evidence that racial anxiety can have a significant negative effect on cross-racial encounters.[3]

Fatigue by People of Color

In recent years, people of color have decreased patience with the task of being the conduit by which racism skeptics are educated about racial dynamics. Working on white folks' racial literacy is often described as performing "emotional labor" for which there is scant compensation. Given the availability of information about racial history and current social and psychological dynamics, it should be understandable that people are less interested in times past in doing this work.

It is important to remember that doing this engagement work is not only time consuming, but also has an emotional toll; this toll is higher for people of color than for white folks. When mobilizing their compassion to engage a racism skeptic without judgment, a person of color must set aside their own frustration or anger that the viewpoints they are confronting have direct negative implications for how they, their family, and their community are being treated. This is arguably more difficult than working through the feelings (admittedly difficult in many cases) that white allies confront when they focus on connecting with the compassion needed when they try to try to reach racism skeptics.

Ethical Concerns

It should go almost without saying that a strong reason for offloading the duty of working with racism skeptics from people of color to white people is an ethical concern. Given that people of color are

---

2   https://igpa.uillinois.edu/programs/racial-attitudes
3   https://www.psychologicalscience.org/publications/observer/obsonline/contagious-anxiety-in-inter-race-interactions.html

directly coping with being the targets of the system of racial oppression, society should not expect them to shoulder the primary burden of persuading people to end this system. This is ethically problematic on its face, especially when there are good-hearted white people who see the same situation and who could be taking on this work themselves.

Does the RACE Method *Enable* White Fragility and White Privilege?

There are people, certainly outside of the Unitarian Universalism and perhaps within it, who argue that using compassion-based ways of engaging racism or denial of it represents a dysfunctional response to white fragility. Some even argue that a allies who use such methods are using their white privilege for the purpose of keeping in place a skeptic's white privilege, in this case, the privilege of not being made too uncomfortable about racism.

This initiative looks at this issue very differently. Here is why:

There is no doubt that empathy and compassion are intended to minimize the effect of white fragility on sabotaging conversations. (One example of white fragility is a conversational response that many white people have that make it difficult to have a focused and reality-based conversation about race.) The methods of this project are structured in a way that tries to steer encounters away from some of the common conversational off-ramps that comprise white fragility.

There are settings when it is useful to vigorously attack white fragility as a problem; there at times when it is useful to call it out, to describe with the sharpest language possible, and to rail against it. For instance, these linguistic strategies can be very energizing at meetings of anti-racism activists where the purpose of the gathering is to mobilize people's energy for the fight against racism and white privilege. However, in the context of a one-on-one conversation with racism skeptics aimed opening up their minds to the idea that racism and privilege matter, such approaches is not likely to be effective, and may even be counterproductive.

The perspective of this project flips on its head the idea that allies using empathy are merely indulging white privilege.

This project encourages allies to ask themselves some difficult questions related to whether it is an act of white privilege to continue to engage in confrontational or avoidance strategies when dealing with racism skeptics. For some allies, encounters like this are invigorating in confirming out rightness or righteousness or have some other emotional payoff. Still, allies must ask themselves whether continuing to pursue these strategies is really an emotional indulgence and whether they should focus on embracing that compassion and empathy, though admittedly this is more difficult, in order to create a better chance of being effective (as well as spiritually more healthy).

Compared with what a person of color might face in the same conversation, it is a form of privilege to hear remarks that deny the existence of racism, and not be reminded of how racism has affected you, your life choices, and your opportunities. It is a form of privilege to be able to hear racist remarks and know that these remarks are not directed at your family, your ancestors (and likely your descendants),

> In fact, it is not white privilege to use compassion and empathy-based strategies. Instead, once an ally knows that compassion is a best practice, it is arguably an act of white privilege *NOT* to use empathy- and compassion-based strategies when talking to skeptics.

and the community you may have come from. It is a form of privilege to look at the changes in racism as something that affects your overall assessment of society's health, instead of something that has implications for the your physical health, safety, and general well-being.

Essentially, white people who are not part of mixed families have the privilege of having some additional emotional distance from the problem of racism. This initiative comes from the position that this additional distance is useful to support people making centered choices in how to engage racially problematic moments. To not do so and to revert back to strategies that are comfortable in avoidance or energizing in confrontation but ultimately ineffective, when you already know that these strategies rarely move the needle, is arguably to shirk the responsibility of leveraging white privilege for social change.

It would be unrealistic to expect that every ally should instantly be able to use empathy-based strategies from just hearing about them. It would also be lacking in compassion to have this expectation and to rub people's noses in their inevitable failures to live up to their highest selves. Clearly, most allies need a good deal of retraining from typical responses, even if these responses are not producing satisfying results. As comrades in the anti-racism community, we must be both compassionate and discerning…with each other and with ourselves. This means asking tough questions about whose interests are being served when an ally chooses to engage in unproductive confrontation or skillful race-conversation avoidance when racially problematic topic with a skeptic comes up.

This project takes the position that when reflecting on a racially problematic encounter with another white person, allies need to ask different questions about the use of their privilege. Today, after an encounter with someone who is racist or racism denying, too many allies reflect on the question by asking themselves: What could I have done to more strongly demonstrate how wrong the person was? It is time that allies start encouraging each other to ask different reflective questions like: How could I have more effectively invited the skeptic to better thinking about race and invited them into another conversation about race, even if that conversation is not with me? Has the encounter I had increased or decreased the likelihood that the skeptic will someday come to a better understanding?

The hope is that the journey through this Boot Camp will train you to ask better questions of yourself and of other allies.

Some Housekeeping Issues Before You Get Started

Stepping Out of Your Comfort Zone

The purpose of this guide is to improve your ability to effectively and compassionately manage conversations with other people. In service of that, you will be guided to execute specific activities that involve interacting with others. If you have a socially isolated life circumstance, (or a very introverted personality), you will face additional challenges in doing the exercises in the guide. These challenges will not be insurmountable; you will simply need to initiate short conversations with people in places like cafes and grocery stores. For the most part, you will be focused on developing your skills in asking questions and listening attentively. If you approach people pleasantly and signal that you only want a short conversation, the vast majority of people will talk to you.

The exercises are all aimed at increasing your ability to engage both people you know and people you don't know in conversations about race/racism. We recognize that engaging people whose

racial views you don't know will feel like a stretch for some people, especially those who lean toward introversion. If you have to push past a disinclination to engage strangers, remember that the core task you are doing is extending compassion, and thus increasing the amount of compassion in the world.

Doing Each Step's Tasks

The vast majority of each step's exercises are designed to take 25 minutes or less per step. One certain exception is step 24, which will likely take about 45 minutes; it will also require you to engage a friend (a Boot Camp Buddy, which will be explained below) to help you. Depending on your reading speed, step 1 may also take you longer than 25 minutes; this step has more reading than any other step of the Boot Camp.

There are many studies that suggest that if you practice a new behavior (including a new thought pattern) for 21 days in a row, you maximize your chances of making it a new habit. Thus, the best way to most effectively use this Boot Camp is to engage the material for 28 days in a row, as outlined. In the testing phase of the Boot Camp, a number of people who were enthusiastic about improving their allyship reported that the demands of life made it virtually impossible for them to actually devote 20 minutes a day to the activities. You might decide that you will more reliably complete the sequence by completing the tasks every two days or at some other frequency. Whether your Boot Camp step is one day, two days, or some other frequency, you will get the best results if you at least think

This RACE Method Boot Camp is formatted to allow for you to take notes on your experience every step. Doing so will significantly aid your progress. But if the time demands of your life make the journaling expectation feel burdensome, it is more important to do the exercises. The ongoing journal entries can partially make up the gap in reflection if you can't make some reflection notes every day.

In addition, please do the tasks of Boot Camp steps in order; they have been sequenced as a progressive behavioral curriculum.

For a few of the exercises, it will be helpful to work with a friend who supports you putting energy into improving your allyship. Early in the process, you will be asked to identify one or two who might serve as your Boot Camp Buddy. It is best if this person is also engaged in this process too, but at a minimum, they need to not oppose this process as an aspect of your personal growth. You should consider keeping them apprised of your ongoing progress on or the step after your regular reflection and synthesis, so they feel connected to and invested in your development.

Structure of This Document

In addition to this Introduction and the Daily guidance that directly follows, this Boot Camp includes an appendix that serves as a Leaders Guide. It contains a variety of guidance and instructions for people who want to lead discussion groups. The Leaders Guide is written with the expectation that group leaders already have some past experience and basic skills in organizing and leading learning groups. The document gives some advice about how someone who wanted to convene a group might think about some important logistical factors that can be critical to group success.

In addition, the Leaders Guide Appendix gives high-level instructions for a group meeting agenda. For each element of the meeting, some learning objectives are discussed, and one or more processes suggested for achieving those objectives.

Differences Between This Edition of the Boot Camp and the 'Generic" Edition

The RACE Method Boot Camp continues to be in demand. The vision of this project is to use tailored approaches that resonate with people in many places so they find this document even more useful to their individual journey toward more effective allyship because of that personalization. This volume is our first exploration into such specialization; one that participants in our workshops or readers of our books have been asking us for.

This document has added a good deal of upfront explanatory material as well as the daily guidance about the relevance of UU spiritual principle. There are a relatively small number of changes to the daily tasks that the reader is instructed to do. The goal was to maintain as much consistency as possible between this Unitarian Universalist version and the original Boot Camp. This will make it easier for learning groups to include people who have the original version and people with this version to be a part of the same discussion group, with minimal adjustments by group leaders.

The places where there is a divergence between the editions will be explicitly discussed in the Leaders Guide Appendix at the end of this document.

*Congratulations on starting
an important journey!*

*"If you want others to be happy,
practice compassion.
If you want to be happy,
practice compassion."
—Dalai Lama*

Step 1

Understanding
The RACE Method Approach

"Racism springs from the lie that certain human beings are less than fully human. It's a self-centered falsehood that corrupts our minds into believing we are right to treat others as we would not want to be treated." —Alveda King

Grounding — 3rd Principle:
Acceptance of one another and encouragement
to spiritual growth in our congregations.

Step 1's Objectives

- Read this overview about the core approach of this initiative.
- Make a list of racially problematic statements you've heard.
- Make a list of people you know with problematic views

This will be the only step in the Boot Camp that will be primarily focused on reading.

Goal

Please make sure that you have read the introduction materials before embarking on this journey as a compassionate warrior. If you follow these exercises and commit to the tasks, you will have transformational experiences — just as in any other Boot Camp. We encourage you to take this on within the supportive community of your congregation or with other committed allies. We have an opportunity to approach the task of engaging skeptics not because we are judging them negatively or because we need them to change in order to feel good about ourselves. Instead, we can choose to engage them because we love and are invested in what could be. While we deeply accept who they are, we choose to try to understand and influence them because we know that if we can find a way to focus on empathy, compassion, and listening, we will both be better off — even if they as skeptics never change their views — because we have an increased possibility of bringing about the change we wish to see in our world: a peaceful and loving society with freedom, liberty, and justice for all. It is from this centered place of love for the world that we start this journey.

This step's tasks are to further familiarize yourself with the methods of this project, and to do some initial thinking about people in your life who in one way or another may positively contribute to your improvement in using RACE Method skills. There will be more reading on this step than any other step of the Boot Camp. The RACE Method Boot Camp is based on the finding that conversational approaches using respectful dialogue, empathy, and storytelling are more effective in influencing others compared with conversational styles that emphasize factual information, debate, combat, and shaming people. A critical task for influencing others is to remain calm and centered, and not emotionally activated when disagreements on the issues occurs. It is valuable to have pre-rehearsed strategies you can use to calm yourself if necessary. It is also helpful to have self-management strategies you can invoke during the conversation to help you regain a centered and calm place if you begin to stray.

In the introduction, a number of findings were discussed from various sciences that point toward compassion and empathy-based methods as best practices in persuasion. In accord with these findings, the ACT Initiative suggests entering conversations about race and racism with racism skeptics with a general sequence and plan of how the conversation might evolve. A key strategy in getting people to revisit their points of view is to first establish a sense of rapport with them and get them to see you as someone who is like them, not someone in an opposing group.

One way of building rapport—even if someone has just made a statement you find problematic—is to ask them to say more about their point of view, even if it's something as simple as saying, "Tell me more about that." Ideally, you want them to do more than restate their belief; you want them to reveal underlying factors, such as their deeper values or experiences. Focusing on values is usually better than talking about beliefs. But even more effective in creating connection is talking about personal experiences. The best strategy is to focus the conversation on the personal experiences that have been notable in shaping or reinforcing their beliefs. Their telling you personal stories is important in firing up your mirror neurons and building a sense of connection. After you have asked for their story and listened empathetically to it, you can take advantage of the reciprocity principle. Even if they tend to be talkative, most people will feel obliged to listen to you if you have listened to them. Now, it is your turn to fire up their mirror neurons by telling a compelling story. To solidify rapport, the first story you tell should be one that they naturally empathize with. Your goal is to get them nodding along with your story and identifying with the idea that you and they have similarities.

After you have further enhanced the sense of rapport, you are in a much better position to try to influence them. Once they trust you and do not see you as the enemy, it is best to relate a personal experience that has influenced the way you see the issue at hand (in this case race/racism). The sequence above can be summarized as **the RACE method of managing a conversation.**

RACE stands for
R: Reflect—get ready for the conversation
A: Ask about their experiences
C: Connect—relate a personal story they will find partially affirming of their viewpoint
E: Expand—relate a personal story that invites them to a new understanding of the issue

This initiative takes the position that of all the many dimensions of the disconnections between white people who see racism differently, there are four deficits among allies that are most important in blocking effective communication.

1. **Allies are not skilled and comfortable in relating stories that might identify areas where the ally himself or herself is still sometimes subject to having their thoughts and/or actions affected by unconscious racial biases.** The fact that few anti-racism allies can talk comfortably about their residual prejudices makes it more possible for skeptics to maintain their denial that racism against POCs is a problem.

2. **Allies are not skilled in telling stories that support the idea that significant racial progress in some dimensions has been made over the past several decades.** This skill has not been developed largely because anti-racism allies fear that making concessions about racial progress will support racism skeptics' denial and minimization of ongoing racism. The inability and/or unwillingness of allies to talk about racial progress over the decades supports the idea among the racism skeptic population that allies are blinded by a "liberal agenda" and cannot see obvious truths.

3. **There is a tendency among many allies to lump together people who deny racism, those who are notably but not extremely prejudiced, and people who are consciously bigoted as all part of "white supremacy" culture.** While there is some truth to this, the lumping together of people at these very divergent parts of the opinion spectrum makes racism skeptics feel like they are not granted any credit for whatever attempts they have made to resist adopting pro-bigotry messages from the culture or people in their personal lives. When people feel as though their decent intentions are not recognized as such, they resist other messages that allies have about the nature of racism.

4. **Many allies can talk about white privilege in a general way, but a much smaller portion have done the reflective work that allows them to talk in a detailed specific and heartfelt way how they personally experience unearned advantages of being a white person in the culture.** As a result, when allies bring up the idea of white privilege, many skeptics feel like they are hearing regurgitations of analysis that the ally has absorbed, instead of a heartfelt reflection of their actual lives. By telling a story that is both specific and heartfelt, the ally will make the idea of racial advantage harder to minimize or dismiss.

A Note About Terminology

- This project divides the population of white Americans (and perhaps others) into two broad categories. People who think that racism against people of color is a problem worthy of addressing specifically are called "anti-racism allies," or merely "allies." Clearly, there is a broad spectrum of intensity, focus, and commitment among allies. Some allies devote their entire lives to promoting racial equity, whereas some are just barely on the good side of the 45%/55% split. Many projects and writers focused on inclusion emphasize these distinctions, such as distinguishing between allies, advocates, accomplices, and activists. In some contexts, these differences are important. Since this Boot Camp focuses on empowering and equipping anyone on the ally side of the divide to more effectively engage racism skeptics, this document will only spend minimal time on categorizing distinctions between different levels of ally-ship.

You will be asked to develop four stories. Two of these stories—one about racial progress and one about knowing a deeply biased person—are intended to build trust with a racism skeptic by conceding two ideas they tend to believe that allies usually are unwilling to admit.

You will also be asked to develop two or three other personal stories, one or two about having racially problematic thoughts yourself, and if you can, one that conveys your awareness of benefiting from white privilege yourself. These are perspectives about race that skeptics are often disinclined to admit. The goal of these stories is to invite the skeptic to empathize with your perspective about your own life, and potentially explore whether there is a way that similar ideas might apply to themselves.

When interacting with racism skeptics, your stories about racial progress and knowing deeply biased people will serve as Connect stories, aimed at building rapport. Your unconscious bias and unearned racial privilege stories will serve as Expand stories intended to invite the skeptic to broader thinking.

Step 1 Tasks

Part 1: Racially Problematic Statements You Sometimes Hear

The exercises in the Boot Camp will not focus on these stories until step 7. But if you want to get started early, feel free to let your mind start percolating on these questions:

- What is a moment you had that demonstrates that you still are subject to thinking thoughts that reflect an unconscious racial prejudice/bias, even if only briefly?

- What is a moment when you observed something that demonstrates to you that there has been notable racial progress in some dimensions in the past few decades?

If you find yourself resisting these ideas, don't worry. We will return to these ideas later. Still, to maximize your experience, we suggest that you assume the questions are based on something that is true, even if part of you wants to raise objections.

What are four statements that you've heard from other white people that you think are racist or racially problematic? Don't describe the statements; write them as you've heard them. Put them in quotation marks.

1.

2.

3.

4.

Part 2: Racism Skeptics in Your Circle of Influence

Think about people in your extended circle of contacts who are likely to be racism skeptics. That is, they would likely be among the 55 percent of white people who would say on an anonymous survey that they think that racism against whites is just as important a social problem as racism against blacks. Also, try to remember something they said that makes you think they are a racism skeptic.

Name of Racism Skeptic:	One statement they made that reflects that they are a skeptic:
1.	
2.	
3.	
4.	
5.	

Part 3: Potential Boot Camp Buddies

Think about two people who can be your Boot Camp Buddy. This is someone who may not be doing the Boot Camp, but who would be supportive of your working on your compassionate communication skills in service of dismantling racism. A few times during the Boot Camp, you will want to borrow a little bit of their time to run stories by them and get feedback. On Boot Camp step 24, you may ask them to do a role play exercise. It is best if both of you are in the same room, but the most important thing is that you have a good relationship that is supportive of your efforts to grow in your allyship.

Potential Buddy #1:

Potential Buddy #2:

Before too long, you may want to talk to your buddies and tell them about your need of their support in the next 29 steps. Once they say they are willing to support you in this way, checking in with them now and then will likely increase their investment in your progress.

Reflection

Take a moment to think about why you want to commit to this Boot Camp. It may be useful to refer to what you write in this space periodically to see if your spirit has shifted along the way.

Closing

"I do not ask the wounded person how he feels, I myself become the wounded person." — Henry David Thoreau

Date: / /

Step 2

Learning Quick Relaxation Methods And Listening Tips

"A mind at peace, a mind centered and not focused on harming others, is stronger than any physical force in the universe." —Wayne Dyer

Grounding — 2nd Principle:
Justice, equity and compassion in human relations.

Step 2's Objectives
- Choose and begin experimenting with a fast-acting relaxation method.
- Choose and begin experimenting with a behavior that enhances your ability to listen.

To make good choices in conversations with skeptics, it is useful to enhance your ability to relax just before or during a tense interaction. In addition, it is useful for everyone to discover techniques that will help them become a better listener.

This step's focus is to begin experimenting with ways of centering yourself in order to create and access the inner peace needed to generously give others room to be their full selves. When we have found calm in the midst of the chaos in our lives and minds, we can experience others without the filters that often cloud our view of other people. Faith traditions from around the world have sought and practiced mind-calming methods. Meditation, yoga, mindfulness, prayer, and many others are all techniques used to bring our minds back to calm balance, especially after being triggered by a negative stimulus.

Our hope is that we can do our small part in creating a world where compassion and equity are the hallmarks of daily life. A key requirement is that we find a way to stop the internal chatter and calm our own heightened fear responses so that we can deeply listen to others and understand the deeper human motivations that unite us. We must do this even when others sometimes say things that make them seem very different than ourselves.

Relaxing our body can help us open our minds and hearts to the experience of others.

Goal

Even if you already have your own rapid relaxation practice, you are encouraged to try some of the ones presented below. The big picture message is this: One factor that will affect your capacity to execute RACE Method is your level of centeredness and relaxation in the face of racially problematic situations. Thus, part of the goal of the Boot Camp is to encourage you to mentally and emotionally link empathetic listening methods with the relaxation methods.

Following are short descriptions of four different relaxation methods that have been promoted as capable of providing benefits after three minutes of engagement. After reading them over, notice which ones you are drawn to. You should first do the one that stands out the most, but we suggest that after a couple of steps, you try some of the other ones. Sometimes people find that a method they did not think would be helpful turns out to be so.

Part 1: Choose a Relaxation Method, Try It, Notice How Well It Works

For all of these exercises, it may be valuable to set a timer for three minutes.

1. **Deep Breathing and Noticing Thoughts**

Get in a relaxed sitting position in the quietest place that is convenient to access. Try to focus on your breathing. When you inhale, think "I am"; when you exhale, think "at peace." As extraneous thoughts come in—and they almost certainly will—notice them, gently push them aside, and return attention to your breathing.

2. **Imagine a Relaxing Spot and Go There**

Pick a setting that you find relaxing, whether it is someplace you have already been or someplace that you can imagine. Spend the first 15 seconds establishing a pattern of relaxed breathing, then close your eyes and shift your attention from your breathing to your preferred location. Imagine as many details as about it as possible, but don't pressure yourself to create the clearest mental picture. Focus on the things about the setting that relax you, whether it's the sights, sounds, smells, sensation of the air, or something else. Imagine that you are there and try to live in the relaxation that this place fosters within you.

3. **Progressive Body Relaxation**

During this exercise, you will slide your attention all over your body. At each major body part, take note of how tense or relaxed the part is and briefly try to relax it. Notice how it feels, then move on to the next. Start with your toes and feet, then move up to your ankle, calf, going ever higher and making sure your focus on both sides of your body.

4. **Self Massage**

(This is from Giovanni Zanoni, Massage Therapist at on-demand massage service, ZenNow.)

Close your eyes. Using your index and middle fingers, make small circles on each temple. Let your fingers walk up your hairline, making small circles along the way, until they reach the middle of your forehead. Then have them travel down until you reach your eyebrow line and make the same circles outward as you head back to your temples. Since hands can carry a lot of tension (especially for heavy keyboarders), do the following: Use the thumb and forefinger to massage the soft area between the thumb and index finger. Do one hand with the other and then switch.

Your task is to choose one of these methods and use it over the next four steps, starting today. Now and at least for the next ten steps, whenever you do one of these relaxation methods, make a note (mental, written, or on a device) about how well the method worked.

Part 2: Review a List of Listening Tips, Then Choose Two to Practice.

Below is a list of Listening Tips that anti-racism allies have said can be helpful when trying to be an empathic listener. This step's list focuses on the mind-body connection. (This is not the last list of tips you will see during the Boot Camp.) Make a note of the two that you think might work best for you.

- Biting your lip
- Touching your tongue to the roof of your mouth
- Shifting your position to one that is more relaxed
- Taking deeper breaths
- Keeping your eyes focused on the speaker's eyes

- Imagining there is glue on your lips, preventing you from talking
- Keeping your eyes focused on the speaker's mouth

If you have a Listening Tip not on this list, be sure to add it. On this step's worksheet, there is a table that can house your reflection notes about how well the listening tips worked in conversations.

Step 2 Tasks

Execution

1. Choose one of the following three-minute relaxation methods:
   - Deep breathing and noticing thoughts
   - Imagine a relaxing spot and go there
   - Progressive body relaxation
   - Self-massage

2. Execute the method, and make a mental note of the answers to these questions:
   - What is your level of relaxation/tension at the start of the exercise?
   - How much did the exercise help you move toward greater relaxation?
   - Note any other observations about the experience of using the method you use.

3. Choose two of the following Listening Tips to use:
   - Biting your lip
   - Touching your tongue to the roof of your mouth
   - Shifting your position to one that is more relaxed
   - Taking deeper breaths
   - Keeping your eyes focused on the speaker's eyes
   - Imagining there is glue on your lips, preventing you from talking
   - Keeping your eyes focused on the speaker's mouth
   - (Your own tip)
4. Try one tip at two different conversational opportunities

Assessment

	Topic & Person	My listening performance from (lowest) 1 to 10 (highest)
Which Listening Tip_____		
Which Listening Tip_____		

Which of these best describes the impact of the Listening Tip on your performance as a listener?

	Listening Tip 1 _____	Listening Tip 2 _____
Very helpful		
Somewhat helpful		
Not helpful/Not distracting		
Somewhat distracting		
Very distracting		

Reflections

How well did the relaxation methods work?

What are your key takeaways from your experience with them?

How did the listening tips work?

Key take aways from your experience of them?

Closing

**It is better to conquer yourself than to win a thousand battles.
Then the victory cannot be taken from you.
— Buddha**

Date: /   /

Step 3
Asking Questions That Focus On Experiences Beneath Beliefs

"If you do not know how to ask the right question, you discover nothing." —W. Edwards Deming

Grounding - 4th Principle:
A free and responsible search for truth and meaning.

Step 3's Objective:
* Ask two people to relate experiences they've had that affect their beliefs.

In order to come closer to the deeper truths of life, it is vital that we go beyond our own perspective and experience. We can't possibly know everything, so we must be committed to learning from others. Unfortunately, our natural tendency is to gravitate toward people in our own tribe with whom we have things in common. These comfortable connections with others help us feel settled, but if we seek truths that are truly transcendent, we must be expansive in our search. To find the connecting thread that links us all, we must be willing to engage others whose circumstances landed them in a different tribe.

When we do that, we will often find that they have very different beliefs about themselves and about the world. This should not really be surprising because the circumstances of their tribe have been different from ours, yet the nature of making sense of the world means that we generalize. As we search for what connects us, try to step inside their world as much as possible. Do your best to walk down their path with them. As part of the quest to find the connecting links, learn to ask them to tell us the stories that shaped who they are. It is these stories that help us walk in each other's shoes and feel more compassion for each other's path. A core task within the RACE method is asking people questions to get them talking about their experiences. By the end of the Boot Camp, this should be easy. We will start this step with beliefs that are NOT ones you disagree with.

Goal
* Your goal this step is to ask at least two people about an experience that might lie beneath a belief they have.
* If in your typical day you have encounters that could accommodate people sharing a brief anecdote with you, then just look for those opportunities.
* If in your typical day you do not have encounters with people that could accommodate brief storytelling, you may need to go out of your way to create such an encounter. Before you ask people for an experience that lies beneath their belief, you may need to remind them of a previous conversation when they revealed this belief to you.

Please note: The exercise is still valuable if the belief you ask about is not about race. In fact, you may want to purposely ask about a belief that is about something very benign and not likely to get their or your emotions going. The point of this step is NOT to get into an exchange about race relations; it is to give you practice in directing someone's attention in a conversation from their belief to an experience that is related to that belief. (This is also an opportunity to practice one or more Listening Tips and take note of their impact on you.)

Two Common Ways of Asking Experience Questions

- Asking about a recent experience that validates their belief: "I find that viewpoint interesting. Can you tell me about a recent experience you had that confirmed for you this way of seeing things?"
- Asking about a past and formative experience that helped form their belief: "I was thinking about that conversation we had last week. Remember when you told me that you think (blank). Can you tell me when you first started thinking that way and what you experienced that caused you to realize that? I would love to hear about that."

Step 3 Tasks

Planning

- Say each of the question types out loud twice in the mirror to find a way of phrasing them that feels natural.
- Decide whether you might need to make a specific effort to contact people or if your regular life will likely provide opportunities to ask about experiences.
- If necessary, mentally clarify whom you might specially contact and think about how and when you might do that. Think about the topic you want to ask them about.
- Think about which Listening Tip you will use when it's time to listen to the answer to your question.

Execution

- If possible, ask someone for an experience twice during the encounter. If you can, use both the recent and formative experience ways of asking strategies.
- When the moment arrives, use one of the listening tips presented in step 2.
- Notice how comfortably you can pose each of the question types.
- When the moment is over, make a mental (or written) note about your experience.

Reflections

On a Scale of 1-10, how well did you:

	Recent Experience Question	Formative Experience Question
Ask the Question		
Use a Listening Tip		
Make the Person Feel Heard		

Closing

Do you not know that when you love someone, you love the whole of mankind? Do you not know how dangerous it is to love man? Then, there is no barrier, no nationality; then, there is no craving for power and position, and things assume their values. Such a man is a danger to society." — Jiddu Krishnamurti, _The Book of Life: Daily Meditations with Krishnamurti_

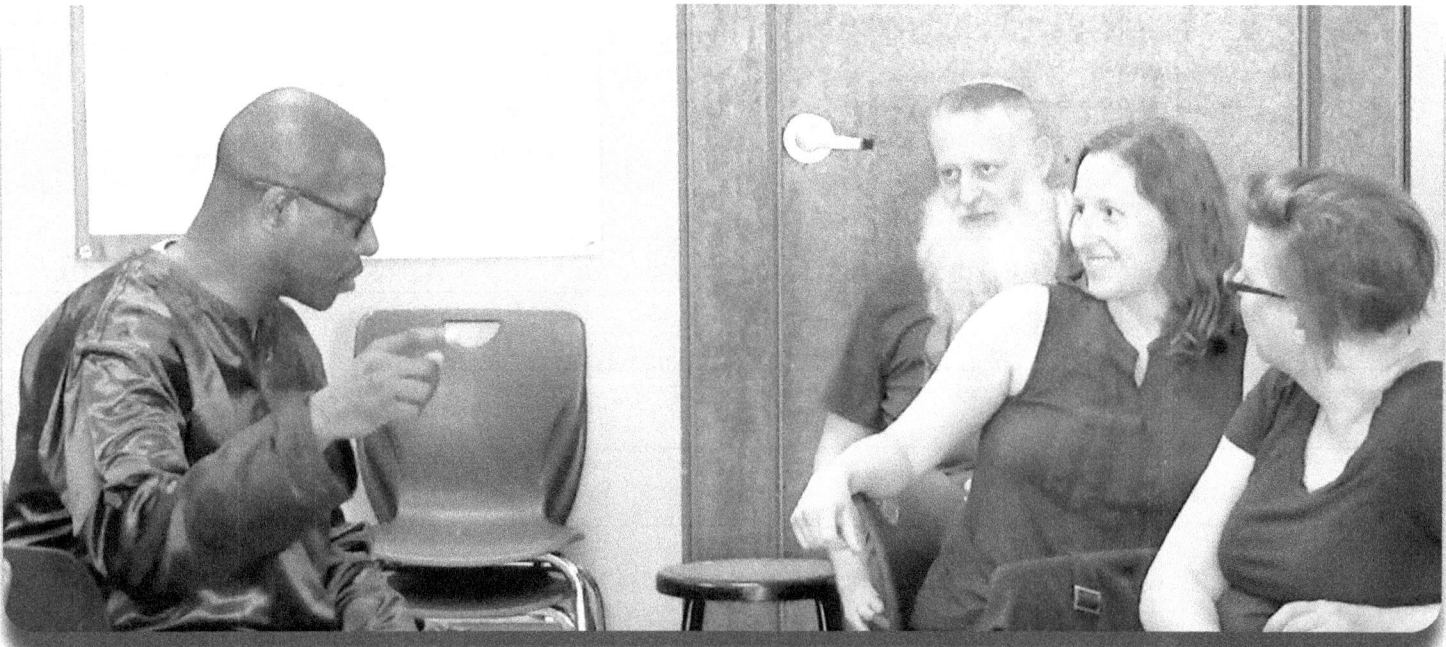

Step 4

The Apologetic Non-Apology

"It is wrong and immoral to seek to escape the consequences of one's acts." — Mahatma Gandhi

Grounding — 7th Principle:
Respect for the interdependent web of all existence of which we are a part.

Step 4's Objective

- Learn about a conflict resolution tool called the Apologetic Non-Apology (ANA)
- Make some initial planning steps in anticipation of doing an ANA

Unitarian Universalism (and some other liberal faith traditions) are covenantal, meaning that the religion exists between the people in how they interact and the agreements they make about how to treat one another. This step we will focus on a method for healing a relationship that has suffered some damage due, in some measure, to things that we ourselves have done or thought. To be motivated to address our role in causing relational damage is inherently to acknowledge the importance we place on the relationship.

Whether it is a close family member or a person with whom our interaction is merely cordial, our desire to smooth the rough waters of a prior interaction recognizes that the most important parts of our lives are relational. We can fuel our souls and provide important spiritual sustenance by nurturing and maintaining healthy relationships. Thus, when disruptions take place, we have two choices: ignore them and experience a rift or take responsibility for our role in disrupting the relationship. By choosing the latter, we honor the interconnectedness our relationship embodies by apologizing without turning the apology into an exchange. Discomfort in talking about race has harmed many relationships between anti-racism allies and racism skeptics. There are people who don't go to family gatherings to avoid repeating a past contentious conversation about race! It is time to heal such breaches.

One key task of Compassionate Warriors is learning and mastering skills for being an active agent of healing where there has been tension or a disruption in the past. When these disruptions happen, there is usually one person who is more at fault, but everybody plays a role. It is particularly important that we are able to hold ourselves accountable for things that we ourselves have done to harm relationships, even if an objective analysis would assess our behavior as having the smaller portion of the blame for the disconnect.

The good news is that we can often initiate a healing process simply by owning up to our piece of the problem, regardless of what the other person does.

Goal

This step is the first of several sessions during the Boot Camp in which you will make progress on something called the Apologetic Non-Apology (ANA). This method of conflict resolution is a way of calling ourselves back into a relationship with someone who is important to us, or with whom we have a vested interest in being in relationship with. (Like all the methods in the Boot Camp, we will not jump into the deep end of the pool right away. We will start slowly and make incremental progress.) The ANA represents a statement where the speaker 1) conveys misgivings about their role in a previous encounter, 2) conveys whatever vulnerability they feel in the moment as they have the conversation, and 3) expresses a commitment to try to avoid repeating this behavior.

When doing an ANA, Compassionate Warriors hold themselves accountable for the behavior in the past that was not helpful to connectedness to the other person. But the person doing the ANA does not issue an apology, nor try to extract an apology from the other person. Apologies are important in healing relationships. However, managing an apology transaction has complications; such interactions can go off the rails and wind up re-injuring relationships. An ANA involves one person simply holding themselves accountable for their misdeeds, without the expectation that the other person will admit anything. Thus, this process has much less risk of causing unintended negative outcomes.

The ANA Has Three Elements:

1. **Past/Accountability:** Recall the topic of the previous conversation and name the behavior (potentially including your thoughts they don't know about) that was not helpful to building a connection with the person. This may be as subtle as mentally labeling someone's point of view "silly" during the conversation.
   Examples of ways to describe your unhelpful behavior:
   •**Superior** •**Dismissive** •**Accusatory** •**Rude** •**Not Listening**
   •**Withdrawn** •**Petulant** •**Talked Over You** •**Acted Like A Know-It-All**

2. **Present/Vulnerability:** Name an emotion based in vulnerability that you are feeling in the moment as you refer to this prior incident
   Examples: •**Embarrassed** •**Nervous** •**Anxious** •**Ashamed**

3. **Future/Commitment to Improvement:** State your commitment to not repeating the problematic behavior. As an optional additional step, you can get the other person's buy-in by asking if it is okay if you ask them about their experience if the topic comes up again.
   Note: you are highly unlikely to get a "no'" answer to this question.

Two Examples of What an Apologetic Non-Apology Might Sound Like Are Below:

Bold indicates the key elements of the ANA.

ANA Example #1

Remember two weeks ago at the barbecue when we talked about the NFL players? I was thinking about it and I realized that I was **dismissive** of your perspective. I actually feel **a little embarrassed** now when I think about this. Our relationship does not need that, so **if we talk about the NFL players protest again, I am not going to act in this way.** Also, is it okay if I ask you about your personal experiences that are related to your viewpoint?

ANA Example #2

A few months back we were talking about poverty, and I was recalling that conversation recently. I realized that during that conversation **I talked over you a lot.** I have to admit that **I am somewhat nervous** just bringing this up now. I want to say that **I don't plan to do that in the future**, and I want to say that if we ever talk about that topic again, I will try to ask you about what you have seen that makes you see the situation like you do. Is that all right?

Note that the ANA does not have to be about race/racism. The conversation that your ANA revisits can be about any topic where you took actions or had thoughts that were unhelpful to your connectedness to someone.

Step 4 Tasks

Preparation

The first step in delivering an Apologetic Non-Apology (ANA) is to prepare for it in advance. It is useful to be as clear as possible about the topic you were discussing, what you did that tended to harm connectedness, and how you think you will feel about it when you bring the prior moment up to the person you were talking to.

By the end of the Boot Camp, you will be encouraged to do an ANA with someone with whom you have had a difficult conversation about race. That is the end of our on-ramp; this step is just the beginning.

For this step, the task is to think about someone with whom you have done or thought something unhelpful to connectedness in a non-racial conversation. You will also answer the following questions and then practice saying the ANA in the mirror.

Question 1: What was the conversation about?

Question 2: How would you characterize the behavior, thoughts, or action that you engaged in? How did they affect the connectedness the two of you share?

Question 3: How do you imagine you will feel when you actually **do** the ANA with the person? *You can complete the ANA by simply declaring your commitment to not doing the unhelpful behavior again. The next question is for situations where you want to go further with getting your conversation partner's buy-in by asking them if it is okay to handle a future conversation differently.*

Question 4: How would you form a question that lets them know that in the future, you would like to ask them about their experiences related to the topic?

Execution

After jotting down answers to these questions, practice the ANA in the mirror.

	Incident 1/Person 1	Incident 2/Person 2
Topic		
What do you think you did that undermined making a connection?		

	Incident 1/Person 1	Incident 2/Person 2
How you think you will feel when talking about it?		
How you would describe what you don't want to do again?		
How would you phrase the questions to get permission to ask about their experience if the topic comes up again?		

Reflection

What was your emotional reaction as you answered the preparation question?

Bonus

There is an Apologetic Non-Apology video explanation and example on the ACT website.

Closing

"But these are just words. The hymns we sing are just songs. All our reflections are just idle thoughts. When we convert them all into loving and responsible action throughout the week, then and only then will this (day) become what we want it to be."
— Robert F Kaufmann 1997

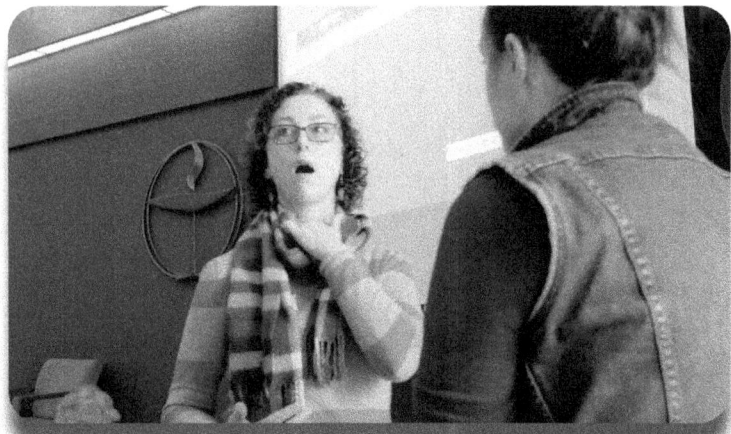

Date / /

Step 5

Focus On Your Connection With Skeptics In Your Circle

"Every problem emerges from the false belief we are separate from one another, and every answer emerges from the realization we are not."
—**Marianne Williamson**

Grounding — 1st Principle:
The inherent worth and dignity of every person.

Step 5's Objective:
- Spend time thinking about your sense of connectedness with people you know who are racism skeptics. *(If you don't know any full-blown skeptics, you can focus on people who whose views on race trouble you.)*

A core tenant of every religion is that each human being has a value that needs to be honored by all others. In the day-to-day realities of life, we sometimes struggle to keep this idea in the foreground of our consciousness.

Connecting our love for humanity with the appreciation for specific people can especially be a challenge when the people in question are those in our circle whose views we find objectionable. But knowing the less polished parts of them should not keep us from feeling the core human-to-human appreciation we should have of them as another child of the universe.

Every human being deserves our love and compassion...even folks who have parts of themselves that we really don't like. If we have trouble finding that love and compassion, the problem is not with them — our job is to keep looking within ourselves.

Goal

As discussed on step 1, the RACE method is based on influencing people by building rapport with them, then inviting them to revisit some of their racial views. To do that, it will be important to get past the natural inclination of many allies to focus exclusively on the ways they feel disconnected from racism skeptics. A step in this direction is to simultaneously hold in your mind their problematic beliefs along with things about them that might enable you to make a connection. That is this step's assignment.

Step 5 Tasks

Review your list from step 1 of the racism skeptics in your circle. *(Some previous Boot Camp participants have said they do not have any skeptics in their circle. If this applies to you, for this step and until the end of the Boot Camp, let the term "racism skeptic" stand for allies whose views on race don't quite agree with yours.)* From your list, choose the two skeptics whose views bother you the most. It is important to choose two people for the exercise.

Do Your Best to Answer These Questions for Both Skeptics

Do One Person at a Time.

1. Identify the groups your skeptic seems to have the most prejudice against. *(If the person is not a skeptic, write down the two specific racial issues in which their views are most problematic to you.)*

2. What is an example of something they said that really bothered you?

3. What are one, two, or three other issues on which their views bother you?

4. Think of the moment when you felt close to them.

5. Think of three things that you would say are admirable about them.

6. Think of three things that you have in common with them.

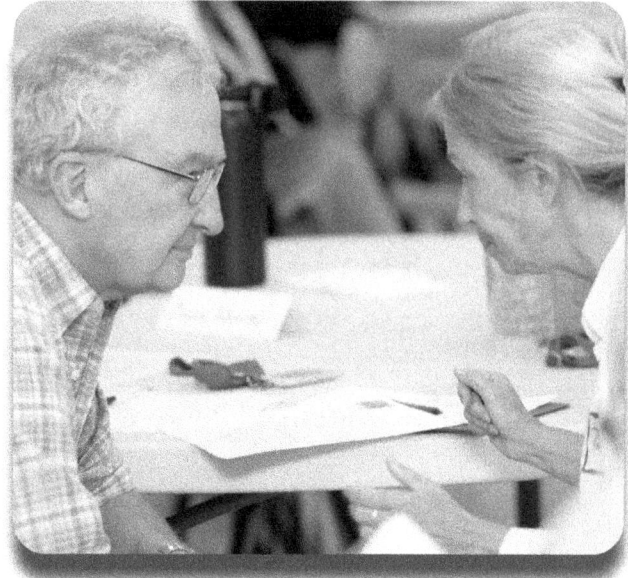

Bonus Question

7. Can you think of something that you did during a race/racism conversation with this person where you did or thought things that were unhelpful to establishing or maintaining connectedness? Jot a few notes down about this moment. *(We will come back to this before the end of the Boot Camp.)*

Step 5 Worksheet

Name of Skeptic:	Name of Skeptic:
Groups they seem to have the most prejudice against:	Groups they seem to have the most prejudice against:

Example of something they said that bothered you:	Example of something they said that bothered you:
If they exist, what are other issues in which their views bother you? *Note if you don't know if they have any other views that trouble you.*	If they exist, what are other issues in which their views bother you? *Note if you don't know if they have any other views that trouble you.*
A phrase or sentence that refers to the time you felt closest to them:	A phrase or sentence that refers to the time you felt closest to them:
What are three things that are admirable about this person?	What are three things that are admirable about this person?

If you can't think of actual racism skeptics, focus on people whose views on race bother you, even though they might be allies.

Reflections

How easy or difficult was it to fill out the worksheet? Were some parts of it more difficult to complete than others?

What thoughts or emotions came up for you as you completed the questions?

Did answering the questions change your perspective about having a conversation with the skeptics?

Closing

**"Never look down on anybody
unless you're helping them up." — Jesse Jackson**

Date / /

Step 6

Finding Ideas You Like Embedded Within Perspectives You Don't Like

"May I find the serenity of mind to accept the things about myself that can't be changed, the strength to change the things that can be changed, and the wisdom to know the difference." — Andrew Newberg

Grounding — Stone 5:
Liberalism holds that the resources (divine and human) that are available for the achievement of meaningful change justify an attitude of ultimate optimism.

Step 6's Objectives
* Watch a news channel with a perspective you disagree with for at least 10 minutes.
* Write down a point of agreement you have that is embedded within a perspective that is expressed on the news channel.

It is quite easy to consign people with racially problematic views to the ranks of the mean-spirited and/or foolish. Given that there is an entire messaging infrastructure that supports thinking that we oppose, many people simply turn away from these messages and retreat to our own information silos that confirm what we already believe. These behaviors by people on both sides have led to our deeply divided society. We must remain optimistic that those of us committed to justice and equity can still make progress by engaging people with whom we disagree.

The challenge is to look for ideas that might be potential sources of connection and common ground. It is vital that we begin this task, which may feel frustrating and even personally sullying, by connecting with our sense of optimism. We must be like the prospectors who looked through a lot of mud to find the occasional gold nugget. To sustain us, we must fill ourselves with the sense that this search for treasures is not in vain, and that the search through noxious material for those camouflaged points of connection is part of our personal journey toward connectedness and ultimately wholeness. Our beloved community is supposed to be radically inclusive.

A key skill for Compassionate Warriors is training the mind to find at least one idea within someone's perspective that you can agree with and use to build rapport. This is the first of a few steps during the Boot Camp for practicing this skill.

Goal

The RACE method is the core of the RACE Method. This method of managing a conversation is based on the strategy of emphasizing at least one point of connection/agreement with a racism skeptic before trying to invite them to a new way of thinking. Because you have a sense of the kinds of statements you hear most frequently or that bother you the most, you can prepare in advance for these encounters. A useful task is to review specific racially problematic statements and clarify ideas within them that you can align with.

Even if you do this, racially problematic statements will come up that you don't expect, so it is important to be able to respond in the moment. This step's exercise attempts to begin training your brain to look for some idea embedded in a perspective you disagree with and find something you can agree with.

One participant has described this process as "looking for the chocolate in the trail mix."

When engaging someone who has said something that you find problematic, finding that chocolate in the trail mix means finding one statement that might allow you to say: "I may not agree with (problematic idea), but I do share your belief that (embedded point of agreement).

Here are a few examples from the White Ally Toolkit and from fall 2018 headlines:

- "I may not agree that very few people are racist anymore, but I do share your belief that a lot fewer people are explicitly bigoted than a few decades ago."
- "I may not agree that police always treat people fairly, but I do share your belief that there are many good police officers out there."
- "I may not agree that Brett Kavanaugh is suitable for the Supreme Court, but I share your belief that every allegation against a nominee for an important position must not be automatically believed as true without investigation."
- "I may not agree that separating families at the border is a good idea, but I share your belief that it would be unwise to have a policy of completely open borders."

Note: These examples are not meant to imply that you need to agree with these specific embedded points.

Step 6 Tasks

1. Spend 10 to 15 minutes taking in a national news roundup on a network that you tend to disagree with. If you are a progressive, Fox News Channel will likely serve the purpose. If you a centrist or conservative, MSNBC or a show like Democracy Now will work well.

2. As you listen, try to distill an important belief that is behind a story. THE IDEA DOES NOT HAVE TO BE RACE RELATED. This should be a perspective that you think most fans of the show would unabashedly agree with.

3. Try to find an idea that is embedded within this perspective that you can agree with. Write down the idea in the previously mentioned format: "I may not agree with XXXX, but I share your belief in YYYYY."

Pay attention to whether any emotions come up for you as you do this exercise. If they do, make a note of them. Remember, this does not have to be a racial issue for you to get value from exercising your brain in this way.

Step 6 Worksheet

- Take in information from a news roundup that is from a source that you usually disagree with.
- Listen carefully for 10 to 15 minutes. Jot down editorial perspectives within the stories that you tend to disagree with.
- Try to find at least one idea embedded within the perspective that you find agreement with.

Perspective you disagree with #1 *I do not agree that:*	Embedded idea you agree with #1 *But I do share the belief that:*
Perspective you disagree with #2 *I do not agree that:*	Embedded idea you agree with #2 *But I do share the belief that:*

Reflections

Did you have any reaction to doing this exercise that is worth noting?

Are there racially problematic statement issues you hear that you cannot imagine finding some embedded ideawith which you can align?

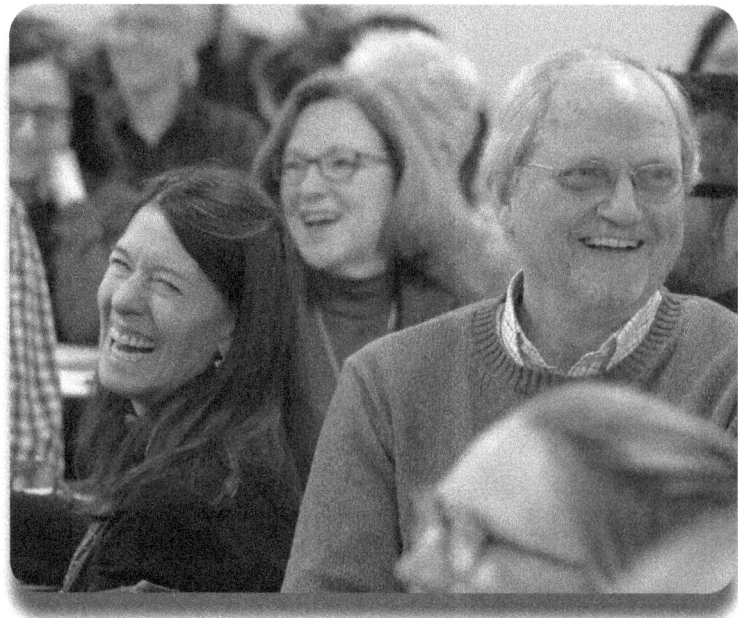

Closing

"He who cannot put his thoughts on ice should not enter into the heat of dispute." —Friedrich Nietzsche

Step 7

Your Experience Of Unconscious Bias

Opening Words: *"Yesterday I was clever, so I changed the world. This day I am wise, so I am changing myself."* — **Rumi**

Grounding — Stone 1:
"Religious liberalism depends on the principle that 'revelation' is continuous."

Step 7's Objective
- Read some background information about unconscious bias, and then begin preparing a story about your being a witness to unconscious bias.

Our religious tradition is a living tradition because we are always learning new truths. At our core nature, human beings are good. Unfortunately, human beings have created systems and structures that are not. We can believe humans are good while simultaneously recognizing that if we want to create a better world, we must actively engage to change systems. Engagement is not just about trying to move others towards enlightenment. We must also be committed to our own constant development—our journey towards wholeness which is ongoing and never ending. Remember, our inherent goodness does not prevent us from participating in systems that are harmful to others, nor does it stop us from absorbing thoughts and feelings from our daily lives and lived experiences that do not reflect our higher human qualities of love and generosity; therefore, we must actively identify and wrestle with fears, prejudices, and other thoughts that interrupt our progress toward effective allyship. Interruptions create divisions but our covenant challenges us to come back into relationship and balance, both with others and ourselves. This work is uncomfortable and difficult, but also rewarding.

This recognition of the need for us to not rest in our own goodness but to energetically strive to improve can help fuel a courageous look at evidence of our own biases, which is the task for this step.

Goal

A key part of your toolkit as an anti-racism ally is being able to tell a compelling anecdote in which you witnessed a moment when a white person was operating on an unconscious racial bias. It is best— although not absolutely necessary—if that person is you. This step's task is to start developing this key tool in your toolkit. To help get you started on developing your tool, this step's assignment contains a greater amount of reading than is usually the case.

ACT has engaged more than 2,500 people in workshops since spring 2017. During that process, we've found that most white allies have witnessed unconscious bias. They are uncomfortable talking about it, but an important step to unlocking your memories is changing from thinking that having a bias is a moral crime to accepting it as an inevitable part of modern life. The consensus among researchers who study unconscious bias is that **the most important step in getting past bias is to admit to yourself that you have it**.

Fortunately, there has been an explosion of written and online resources about this issue in the past few years. For those who need a primer on this topic, one contribution by the ACT team is *Overcoming Bias*, by Tiffany Jana and Matthew Freeman (both Tiffany and Matthew have collaborated with ACT).

Most anti-racism allies are reasonably familiar with some basic facts about unconscious bias, the most important of which is that unconscious bias based on group membership is such a widespread phenomenon that it might be thought of as universal.

A core challenge when discussing bias with skeptics comes from the way that "racism" and "prejudice" are thought about, which is that they only reflect conscious and intentional bigotry. Since relatively few people harbor such feelings, many people proclaim themselves bias-free because they do not understand that bias can be unconscious and nevertheless affect their thoughts and behavior.

Making matters worse, since they don't see any conscious bigotry in their own hearts and minds or in the people they know, many people extrapolate that society is now essentially free of prejudice and racism. Thus, they process claims about racism as so much whining and excuse making, or even as cynical attempts to extract concessions and resources made by people who don't want to work hard.

One reframe of discussions about bias that is often productive is to make the case that people often have unconscious bias against their own group. This reframe makes bias not a function of group animus, but rather an insidious societal force that affects everyone.

Here are some brief pieces of data that illustrate the fact that unconscious bias can push people to have negative views of others in their own group.

- In one study, approximately 1,200 university professors (800 male, 400 female) who ran science labs were sent a resume of a hypothetical applicant for an entry-level lab assistant position. They were asked to rate the competence level of the applicant on a scale from 1 to 5 and to list the appropriate starting salary. All the scientists were sent the exact same resume, except that half of the applicants were named Jennifer Smith and half named John Smith. Overall, John's projected salary was 15% higher than Jennifer's, and his competence assessment was 20% higher than Jennifer's. Significantly, there was no appreciable difference between the ratings by the female and male professors on the level of anti-female bias.[1]

- In an analysis of the Implicit Association Test—an online test of unconscious association—about 29% of African Americans demonstrated an easier ability to associate white faces with positive attributes than black faces. (The portion of whites with a similar characteristic is over 48%.)[2]

- In a 2010 study of 133 children that was sponsored by CNN, children ages four to five and nine to ten were shown images of white-skinned and brown-skinned dolls and were asked to associate them with positive and negative words. (This was a reprise of a famous 1947 doll study by Dr. Kenneth Clark.) Both white and black children showed a significant preference for white dolls.[3]

- The following is a quotation from Jesse Jackson from the mid-1980s where he reflects on the way that he is subject to having an anti-black bias. "There is nothing more painful to me at this stage

1   John Vs. Jennifer: A Battle of the Sexes, Yale Scientific Magazine, February 19, 2013. http://www.yalescientific.org/2013/02/john-vs-jennifer-a-battle-of-the-sexes/

2   Exploring Racial Bias in Single Race and Biracial Adults: The IAT, Pew Research Center, August 19, 2015. https://www.pewsocialtrends.org/2015/08/19/exploring-racial-bias-among-biracial-and-single-race-adults-the-iat/

3   Atlanta Journal Constitution, Mamie and Kenneth Clark used toys in a test that helped to overturn U.S. school segregation law, Feb. 1, 2019. https://www.ajc.com/news/mamie-and-kenneth-clark-doll-test-challenged-attitudes-segregation/gGknWIaYpKa1Yh9Oqs6hjL

in my life than to walk down the street and hear footsteps... then turn around and see somebody white and feel relieved."[4]

At some point, it may be useful to cite such facts in your attempt to influence a racism skeptic to believe that unconscious bias is a real factor. However, do not make the mistake of making facts into your core persuasive strategy. What is more effective is your own personal testimony about your witnessing a situation in which you saw unconscious bias at work. Most effective will be a story where the person having this bias is you.

This step's task is to take some notes about a few incidents when you observed that unconscious bias might have been at work. In several steps, you will turn one of these incidents into an anecdote that you will polish, practice, and at some point convey to others.

Step 7 Tasks

Take some notes in response to these questions. It is not necessary to develop a full anecdote; for the moment, it is fine right now to simply write enough to remind yourself of each incident. Later in the Boot Camp, you will review this list and choose one or more of these incidents to develop a full anecdote.

1. Can you think of an experience where an unconscious or semi-conscious negative racial bias affected your own thoughts or actions—even if only very briefly—in a way that was out of alignment with your values?

Incident #1 when you think a negative racial bias was affecting your thoughts/actions?	Incident #2 when you think a negative racial bias was affecting your thoughts/action?

(If you have notes on two incidents, you can stop here, though we recommend you finish the form if you have enough time. If you don't have two incidents, continue completing the rest of the form.)

2. Can you think of an experience when someone behaved toward you in a way you did not like and that you think was affected by an unconscious racial bias?

Incident #1 when you were the target of unconscious racial bias.	Incident #2 when you were the target of unconscious racial bias.

---

4   The Baltimore Sun, Jesse Jackson's Message Is Too Advanced for Most, December 3, 1993. https://www.baltimoresun.com/news/bs-xpm-1993-12-03-1993337169-story.html

3. Describe one or two incidents when someone behaved toward you in a way that you did not like and that you think reflected an unconscious bias that was not based on race— perhaps gender, age, location, accent, nationality, or something else.

Incident #1 when you were the target of unconscious non-racial bias.	Incident #2 when you were the target of unconscious non-racial bias.

4. Have you ever you observed an interaction between two or more people where you think that unconscious bias (racial or not) was affecting the interaction?

Incident #1 when you observed bias operating between others.	Incident #2 when you observed bias operating between others.

Reflections

Did you have any emotions of note while reviewing your experience and looking for bias?

What are your other observations or lessons from participating in this?

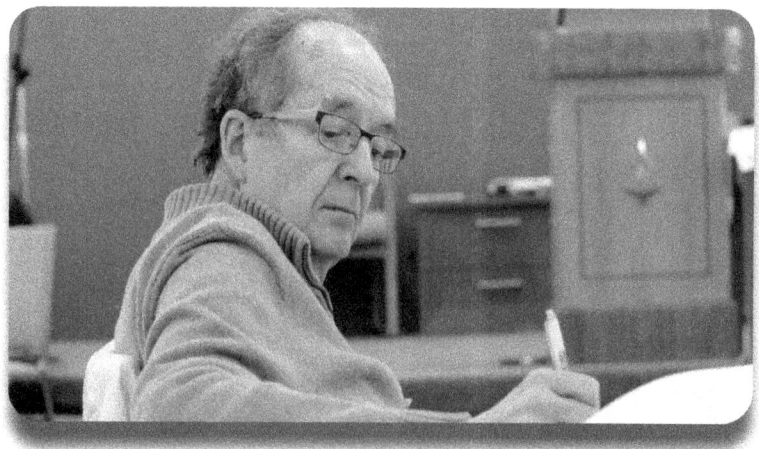

Closing

"Fortunately for serious minds, a bias recognized is a bias sterilized." — Benjamin Haydon

Step 8

Reflection And Synthesis

It's on the strength of observation and reflection that one finds a way. So we must dig and delve unceasingly." — Claude Monet

Grounding — 4th Stone:
We deny the immaculate conception of virtue and affirm the necessity of social incarnation. Good things don't just happen, people make them happen.

Step 8's Objective
- Create written answers to the following questions.

Transformational work is not only ongoing and difficult, it is exhausting. We need to take time regularly to immerse ourselves in intentional reflection: What have we learned? What have we let go of trying to learn? Where are we now? As become better allies, we must find a good balance between the wisdom that comes from action and the wisdom that comes from reflection. If we are only active and never stop to reflect, we may repeatedly make mistakes and choose actions that never move toward betterment. But if we spend too much time in reflection and very rarely act, we can correctly be accused of being self-absorbed navel gazers.

We should choose the middle path, which means stopping on a regular basis to honestly and courageously examine both the impact of our actions and the internal thoughts and feelings associated with them. The search for truth is not predictable. We need to stay ever alert for revelations, which will sometimes come amidst the noise and sometimes in the quiet. Be careful to create the quiet.

Reflections
If you had to present it in a nutshell, what would you say you have learned about:
Your relaxation practices?

Your listening inclinations?

Your relationship with racism?

Your ability/willingness to search for agreement with those with whom you disagree?

Your perspective on unconscious bias?

Are there notable insights that you want to keep in mind as you progress to the next steps?

Your actions or thoughts that were unhelpful to establishing or maintaining connectedness?

Closing

"Humility, that low, sweet root, from which all heavenly virtues shoot." — Thomas Moore

Step 9

Experimenting With New Listening Tips

"There are people who, instead of listening to what is being said to them, are already listening to what they are going to say themselves."
— *Albert Guinon*

Grounding — Stone 1:
Religious liberalism depends on the principle that revelation is continuous. Our tradition is a living tradition because we are always learning new truths.

Step 9's Objectives
- Identify and practice two Listening Tips that you will experiment with in the coming steps.
- Engage a person who likely agrees with you and practice attentive listening
- Make note of how the listening tips affected you

Deep within, most of us know that doing our part to create human oneness requires us to move to a greater degree of accepting other people than we do on a moment-to-moment basis. This step's task is about refining our listening practice. As we strive to increase our ability to radically accept others, we must be able to hear and empathize with them when they try to bring us inside their world. We must be able to hear their stories from a centered place that is fundamentally nonjudgmental.

Even though many parts of our culture tend towards the opposite of empathetic listening, the opportunities for us to practice listening are always present. To make the most of these opportunities, it is useful to figure out what actions or practices best help us reconnect to our deeper motivations for listening, which might be defined as creating a world where everyone's story is considered one that matters and is worth hearing.

Note: It is best if you use this step as an opportunity not just to listen attentively, but to practice the skill of taking in someone's point of view and not offering yours in response. To maximize your chance of doing that, the suggestion is that you not focus on a topic that is highly controversial. After the person finishes explaining their experience, you can thank them, and say you want to think about what they have said. If the person appears to feel uncomfortable, offer your perspective, including an experience related to it.

Goal

In previous Boot Camp activities, you were encouraged to use Listening Tips that focused on the mind-body connection. For the next two Boot Camp steps, you are encouraged to practice Listening Tips that focus on managing your own thoughts.

Many people have found these strategies helpful in boosting their own compassion when talking to people they disagree with about controversial topics. The good news is that these methods are compassion boosters in any situation. Thus, you can try them out over the next two Boot Camp steps, even if you don't have conversations with strong disagreement about race/racism.

Here are some methods that ACT initiative participants have said can be useful at the beginning of or during a tough conversation about an issue where there is disagreement. Clearly, these methods can also be used when the conversation is not contentious.

- Mentally picture the person as the vulnerable child they once were.
- Remind yourself that the listening process you are doing is part of a long-term change process.
- Remind yourself of qualities you like about the person you are talking to.
- Think back to a time when you wanted to be listened to. Think about things you have in common with them.
- Think about helpful values you hold, such as empathy, curiosity, and/or patience.

Step 9 Tasks

1. Choose which of the methods for relaxing, asking questions, and maintaining your listening that you will use this step.
2. Sketch out a plan for when you will use that particular method.
3. Execute your plan.
4. Immediately make a mental note of how well the tip worked, and make some more detailed written notes later.

Planning

- Which relaxation method do you plan to use before you approach them?
- Which Listening Tip are you going to do?
- If you have an idea about whom you plan to engage this step, note who they are below.
- Whom do you plan to engage?
- As you try to shift them from belief to experience, do you plan to ask them about a recent experience or a formative experience?

Execution

1. Find two opportunities to engage your Listening Tip.
2. Pay attention to what you are hearing AND the effects of your Listening Tip on you.

Encounter #1

Person you talked with:

Belief you asked about:

How would you describe how you asked them about their experience?

How smooth was your attempt to transition them from belief to related experience?
☐ Very Smooth | ☐ Smooth | ☐ Kinda Smooth/Kinda Clunky | ☐ Clunky | ☐ Very Clunky

How much do you think they felt really heard? They:
☐ Felt very heard | ☐ Felt heard | ☐ Felt kind of heard | ☐ Did not feel heard

Listening Tip Used:
Before the encounter:
☐ Did it | ☐ Kinda did it | ☐ Didn't do it

During the encounter:
☐ Did it | ☐ Kinda did it | ☐ Didn't do it

How much did the listening tip help you?
☐ A lot | ☐ A good amount | ☐ Some | ☐ A little | ☐ None/it distracted me

Encounter #2
Person you talked with:

Belief you asked about:

How would you describe how you asked them about their experience?

How smooth was your attempt to transition them from belief to related experience?
☐ Very Smooth | ☐ Smooth | ☐ Kinda Smooth/Kinda Clunky | ☐ Clunky | ☐ Very Clunky

How much do you think they felt really heard? They:
☐ Felt very heard | ☐ Felt heard | ☐ Felt kind of heard | ☐ Did not feel heard

Listening Tip Used:
  Before the encounter:
  ☐ Did it | ☐ Kinda did it | ☐ Didn't do it

  During the encounter:
  ☐ Did it | ☐ Kinda did it | ☐ Didn't do it

  How much did the listening tip help you?
  ☐ A lot | ☐ A good amount | ☐ Some | ☐ A little | ☐ None/it distracted me

Reflections

How did it feel to approach the conversation(s) with a focus on listening?

How did the experience of engaging people in this way compare to what you expected?

Any other lessons or takeaways from doing the exercise?

Closing

"Be curious, not judgmental." — Walt Whitman

Date / /

Step 10

Listening To Someone You Disagree With

*"There is a difference between listening
and waiting for your turn to speak."* — Simon Sinek

Grounding — 6th Principle: The goal of world community with peace, liberty, and justice for all.
Stone 5: "Liberalism holds that the resources (divine and human) that are available for the achievement of meaningful change justify an attitude of ultimate optimism." Hope.

Step 10's Objectives

- Practice using a relaxation method before a conversation you know may test you.
- Practice asking about the experiences of a person with whom you disagree.
- Practice a Listening Tip and assess its affect on your ability to listen and make someone feel heard.

The divisive energy that seems to pervade our nation and our world is palpable. Still, it is important to reconnect to the hope of unity people of faith have. We imagine the possibility of unity when we are at our best, a vision where everyone is free, at peace, and our society feels just.

While the world is far from this goal, our responsibility is not to fall prey to thinking that the goals of peace, liberty, and justice for all are only shared by people with whom we agree. The inspirational vision that drives us must be one that includes everyone, even people with whom we thoroughly disagree. For now, try to set aside the obvious difficulties we must surmount to achieve this goal…there will be time to attend to those challenges. Start from the standpoint of spirit and will, in which we wish for a world where people with divergent views stand side by side with us. Only then can we move toward manifesting a world where liberty, peace, and justice are felt by everyone.

The only way to have a hope of creating this world is if people who see things very differently listen deeply to each other. As you advance your skills as an ally, remember that people of color and white people see and experience America very differently, and that there was a time when almost no white people gave that a second thought. Now we are pushing for even more white people to be empathetic to systemic oppression. So, try to find the unity beneath disparate perspectives. If we are to create a world that embraces equity, we must listen our way to it. Listening will create a better world.

This step is the first step where you are going to purposefully engage someone with whom you disagree. Your engagement will simply be asking them an experience question about some belief they have, listening to them without arguing, and exiting the conversation.

Goal

The task of this step is to purposely have a conversation with someone who has a belief you disagree with, and to practice asking them for an experience that animates their belief. Of course, you will also practice listening to their experience with the intention of making them feel heard.

It will be important to resist the temptation to have an argument with them about the belief. In fact, they might want to draw you into such an argument.

To increase the chances of you resisting the temptation to argue with them, it is probably best if the topic that you focus on is NOT something that triggers you. It is best to choose a topic with which you hold mildly differing thoughts. This way, you can test how well the relaxation methods and Listening Tips are helping you.

It might be best if the topic is a public issue that you have only moderate concern about. You may also choose an issue you have strong feelings about but is not as weighty; for instance, maybe you know they like a restaurant that you find terrible. The most important thing in this step is to engage the exercise and not avoid doing so because you can't find the perfect issue.

Again, choose a topic and a person who will test your ability to simply listen and not argue, but will not make you feel like you're doing a disservice to yourself or a cause you care about.

Here is a broad outline of how this conversation might go:

You: *(calmly, since you just did one of your relaxation methods)*: Remember when we had a conversation about *(the topic)*.

Them: Yes

You: It came to my mind the other day. I realized that I wanted to ask you more about your experience related to *(the topic)*. I hope that is okay.

Here is my question: *(Here you choose an experience question style [recent or formative]. Use your empathetic inquiry tone of voice, ask a question about a recent or formative experience related to their beliefs about the topic. Then listen with the intention of making them feel heard.)*

Them: *(they tell an experience related to the topic)*

You: I think I get it. Let me feed it back to you. One time, you *(summarize their experience.)* And that experience is related to why you think *(summarize their belief.)* OK, I think I see where you are coming from now. Thanks a lot for that. It really helps me to hear people's experience so that I better understand their perspective on things. Thanks again.

Note: If they push you to try to tell what you believe or the experiences behind it, you may need to say something like this:

You: Thanks for asking about my point of view. I would be happy at another point to talk about my perspective on this issue, including my experiences that led me to see it how I do. But right now, what I really want to do is to focus on your experience, let that wash over me, and not fill my head with my own perspective. Can I get back to you on that at a different time?

Remember: There is a good chance that during or after they tell you their experience, they will make a link to their belief that you will find irrational or otherwise spurious. If this happens, IT IS IMPORTANT TO RESIST THE TEMPTATION TO ARGUE. Prepare in advance for this possibility. Have a plan for the Listening Tip that you will use to stay focused on your goal, which was to practice asking an experience question, practice a Listening Tip, and make them feel heard.

As soon as you can after the encounter, answer the questions on the worksheet.

Reflections

Did you try a relaxation method before the encounter? If so, how much do you think it helped you?

Which Listening Tip(s) did you try, and when did you do them?

Which style of asking questions did you implement? How would you rate the smoothness of your inquiry?

How well did you listen? What lessons do you walk away with about how to improve your own listening practice?

Were you able to resist the inclination to argue? If not, what might you do in the future to resist that temptation? If you did not argue, did you take any measures to help you resist the temptation?

Did you get any value from actually listening to them, outside of strengthening your listening muscle?

Are there any other important takeaways from this experience?

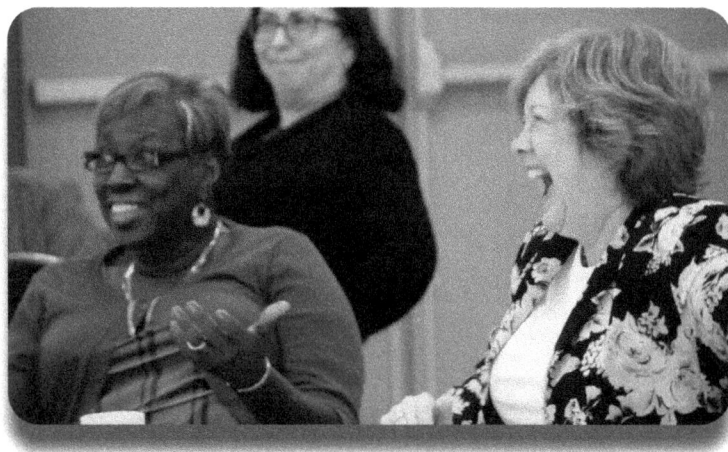

Closing

"Be stubborn about your goals, but flexible about your methods. Be a warrior for compassion, but a lover of all people."
— Anonymous

Step 11

Planning An Apologetic Non-Apology

"A meaningful apology is one that communicates three Rs: regret, responsibility, and remedy." — Beverly Engel

Grounding — Stone 2:
All relations between persons ought to ideally rest on mutual, free consent and not on coercion. We freely choose to enter into relationships with one another.

Step 11's Objective
- Become more comfortable with the Apology Non-Apology (ANA) method

Being in covenantal relationships means that we have to be willing to tend to them. Every relationship will hit a rocky patch once in a while. Committing to heal a relationship that has experienced a rift is divinity in practice.

Remember, the unique approach of the ANA is to make a statement that demonstrates that we hold ourselves accountable for our prior role in undermining the connection with the other person. This is in contrast to an apology, which has a more interactive and transactional connotation. Transactional apologies can also sometimes be vital for relationship healing and often inevitably involve applying subtle pressure on someone to either accept the apology and/or to also return the apology if the other person's behavior played a role in the rift, thus making this transactional. However, in the ANA, the other person does not have to accept, approve, or give permission for you to commit to doing better.

In the ANA discussed here, your statement will not apply any subtle pressure. Instead, you will take full responsibility for your role in the rift. It doesn't even matter if the other person's behavior played a bigger role in the disconnection; what you are doing is holding yourself accountable for what you did or thought that lessened your connection, and committing out loud to a new course of action.

The core sensibility behind this exercise is that there are moments when we should take extra care to avoid manipulating others. Doing so may require us to affirmatively account for our role in a harmed relationship and express absolutely no expectation other than allowing the other person to witness our taking responsibility for our past transgression. Remember, it is only in the giving that we truly learn to receive.

Goal

The goal of this step is to go a bit further than step 4 with the Apologetic Non-Apology. The task is to use the ANA method with someone with whom you have had a disagreement that is not about race.

On step 4, you filled out the ANA for someone with whom you had a disagreement that wasn't necessarily about race. This step's task is to do the same thing, but to choose someone it would not be very difficult to encounter in the course of a typical day.

It is possible that the person you used for your ANA previously is someone you will see in the natural course of the step. If this is true, choose a different person for this step's exercise.

Your goal is NOT to try to create an encounter that has the significance of a deep and weighty apology, but rather is a semi-weighty acknowledgment of an error you committed. The goal is to do a slight reset of your communication pattern, not to perform a big mea culpa.

Think about someone whom you are likely to run across and with whom you have had a conversation in the past year where you did or thought something that was unhelpful to connectedness. When you are clear about your person, use the Worksheet to prepare the ANA and to later capture your assessment of how the experience went.

Step 11 Tasks

To prepare the ANA, answer these questions.

- What was the topic and setting of the conversation where you thought or did something that was detrimental to connectedness?

- What did you think or do that was unhelpful to connectedness?

- How do you imagine feeling as you bring this up?

- What is an honest statement you can make about not doing this again?

- What is an experience question that feels reasonably natural that you might articulate if you wanted to open the topic again?

Think about how to execute this task. These questions might be helpful:

- Will it be helpful to you to consciously relax yourself first? What method will you use?

- Will you need to pull the person aside, or will that add more drama to the encounter than is helpful?

- If they decide to tell their experience of the moment instead of just hearing from you, which Listening Tip will you use so that you make them feel heard?

Now that you have prepared for this encounter, practice the ANA in the mirror.
Do the ANA with a suitable person as soon as you are able.

Reflections

What is your assessment of how the other person felt during and after the encounter?

Is there anything that you might have done differently?

What are the overall lessons from this experience that you want to remember as you think about using this technique in the future?

Closing

Humility is not thinking less of yourself, it's thinking of yourself less.
— C. S. Lewis

Date / /

Step 12

Reflecting On Racial Progress

"The only thing more irritating than white people who say that everything has changed, is black people who say nothing has changed."
— *John Lewis*

Grounding — 3rd Stone:
Religious liberalism affirms the moral obligation to direct one's efforts toward the establishment of a just and loving community. It is this which makes the role of the prophet central and indispensable in liberalism.

Step 12's Objective
- Begin developing your story about racial progress, which will be a connect story for racism skeptics.

Abrahamic faiths teach lessons about the Exodus from bondage into liberation. The stories are timeless inspiration. Thousands of years after Moses led the Jews out of Egypt, we are grappling with the vestiges of slavery in the New World. Thousands of years after Jesus was crucified for proving that neighborly love was more powerful than state rule, we struggle to find time to meet our neighbors or vote. Given the racial and other social hierarchies that continue to plague us, it is easy to fall into despair or frustration about the fact that our nation and world are far from the beloved community and that we will never get to the vision that Martin Luther King, Jr. so eloquently bestowed on our nation in the 1960's. Nevertheless, we must hold on to that vision, and nurture it within us. Keeping this flame of hope alive within us is important in order to remain on the path, but also important for our ability to keep others motivated and actively working toward the society we want and believe to be possible.

In the face of these truths, it is important to take time to appreciate the distance we have traveled already. Though we are far from where we should be, there are millions of people who experience freedoms and a level of justice now that people just like them a few generations ago could only dream of. We should not become complacent, but we should look at the hard-won victories and progress made as a testament to people who were committed to justice and made sacrifices to get us to this point. We must be inspired by these past accomplishments and use them as fuel to keep going.

Now, it is our turn to carry the torch in the march toward a just and loving world, and we need to look in a clear-eyed fashion at both at how far we have come and how far we yet have to go.

Goal

As noted on step 1, this Boot Camp will focus on creating dialogue between allies and skeptics on the race-related issues that create the most common disconnection and disagreement. On step 7, you began to probe your memories for potential stories that showed your connection with the issue of unconscious racial bias. This idea that we all harbor racial prejudices is one that is uncomfortable for white people generally, and particularly so for skeptics. This idea undermines both the idea that racism is over and the notion that a person can just declare themselves innocent of it.

For this reason, stories about these topics will serve as Expand stories that will invite a skeptic to new thinking.

To use the RACE method, you will need to develop Connect stories as well; these stories are intended to nudge the skeptic toward trusting you because it will resonate with their perspective and perhaps experience. Your Connect story will be vital in reinforcing the rapport that you have built by listening to them in the Ask step; the Connect step is important to increase trust and thus the likelihood that they will take your Expand story seriously.

Be warned that Connect stories are usually harder for allies to find the willingness to look for and to tell. As a general matter, the message of a Connect story is that sometimes, race and racism are not the most important factors in situations. While most allies can be pushed to admit that this is true, this idea is not something that allies talk about much; telling stories like this is at odds with the habits of the anti-racism community. This is sensible, since the anti-racism community's purpose is to counter the societal denial about the fact the race and racism are important in a large portion of everyday interactions.

Consequently, for many allies, it feels strange to focus conversational attention on moments when the most important view of a situation is not through a racial lens. To many allies, the idea of purposely leading a conversation toward this idea — especially when talking to a skeptic whose racism denial needs to be opposed — feels like a betrayal, or at minimum, a risky concession that is likely to be exploited.

This view is understandable. To some extent, telling a Connect story is making a concession to the idea that sometimes race and/or racism does not matter. You are making this concession in service of getting the skeptic to agree that sometimes, race and/or racism do matter. Your Expand story is designed to serve as personal testimonial that this is true. The Connect story tells the skeptic that you sometimes see situations as s/he does. The idea is that by time you get to your Expand story, the skeptic will not make a mere rhetorical concession, but will be open to reducing their tendency to deny race /racism, because it will not be hard for them to imagine themselves being in your story and coming to a similar conclusion to yours.

Here is another way of explaining the work underlying the structure of the RACE method and what each story is doing: your Connect story is agreeing with an idea that ideological conservatives tend to think is important — i.e. sometimes people on the left overemphasize race/racism, since sometimes race and racism are not big factors. Your objective in your Expand story is to open their minds to an idea that progressives tend to think is important — i.e. sometimes people on the right underemphasize race/racism, since sometimes race and racism are significant factors.

Over the course of your lifelong allyship, it will be valuable to develop an arsenal of Connect stories, some of which might be very topic-dependent. A Connect story relevant to a conversation about law enforcement might be different than one about white privilege. For now, we suggest that you develop two Connect stories, both of which are designed to nudge a skeptic to trust you and to let down their tendency to be defensive about themselves or about the nation.

The first of these is what might be called a Racial Progress story; this story is one that highlights some improvement in some dimension of racism that you have directly observed. A Racial Progress story conveys the message that you recognize that society is on a path towards improvement. Skeptics often feel that anti-racists refuse to acknowledge their nation's improvement with respect to its racially problematic past. Telling a Racial Progress story is likely to help the skeptic not see you as someone who is hypercritical of the county.

The second type of story (step 20) is also intended to help the skeptic become less defensive, but has a somewhat different focus. On step 20, you will work a story that might be described as a story that conveys "The really bad racist is not here." By telling a story about a person who both you and the skeptic agree has racially problematic views, you will convey that you are giving the skeptic credit for whatever work they have done to resist negative racial messages. This acknowledgment will help the skeptic not see you as not someone who is hypercritical of them.

Step 12 Tasks

Your task this step is to begin developing a story about racial progress that you will at some point use to connect with a racism skeptic. Your goal is to develop an anecdote that reinforces the point that there has been notable progress in recent decades, perhaps even within your lifetime. Look over the following questions and pay attention to which questions resonate with you.

1. If you ever did, when did you first notice that you were receiving messages that encouraged you to see some people of color as "other"? (These messages may have come from family, friends, the media, or other sources). What were some of these messages?

2. What have you experienced that lets you know that there is less bigotry now than there was just after the civil rights movement, or between now and when you were a child? What changes have you seen in your lifetime?

3. If possible, recall a story about witnessing explicit racism that you think would be much less likely to happen these days because of different social norms.

4. Do you have any observations of positive racial trends that you previously witnessed or know of that were less apparent in decades past? (It is OK if these are media observations, such as trends in commercials.) Do you have any observations of negative phenomena that you have observed or know have declined?

5. During your childhood, were you exposed to an adult who tried to teach you to be racist in a way that would not likely happen these days? If so, jot some notes about your memories about this.

6. If you have a secondhand or observational story, from at least 20 years ago, from a person of color who experienced explicit racism in a way that you imagine would be much less likely to happen this step, write down the key elements of that story.

If any of the above prompt questions resonates with you, jot some notes about experiences related to any of the questions that have at least some resonance.

When you are finished with your notes, step away from this task for at least a few minutes. When you return to it, let the memories wash over you again, and put an asterisk next to the two that you imagine most suitable to tell as an anecdote.

Reflections

Did you have any notable reactions — positive or negative — to the assertion that there has been racial progress in recent decades that is notable?

What was your reaction to the idea that allies are often not comfortable talking about racial progress and that talking about this issue is a potential skill for allies?

Are there any other notable takeaways from the experience of reviewing your memory for experiences that suggest racial progress?

Closing

"We shall overcome one day. Deep in my heart,
I do believe, we shall overcome someday."
— African-American Spiritual

Step 13

Turning Notes Into Usable Anecdotes

"Tell me the facts and I'll learn. Tell me the truth and I'll believe. But tell me a story and it will live in my heart forever." — Ancient Proverb

Grounding — 4th Stone:
A free and responsible search for truth and meaning.

Step 13's Objective
- Using your notes from step 7, create an anecdote about unconscious bias.
- Using your notes from step 12, create an anecdote about racial progress.

As people of faith, we aspire both to seek truth and the create justice. In so doing, we must be bold and unflinching by looking courageously under every nook and cranny for pieces of the truth that can help bring ourselves and others closer to the beloved community based on right relations. Our challenge is to have faith that our universal principles will sustain us and keep our actions on the right path.

The right path includes looking into our own personal history, including the moments around which we might have embarrassment or even shame. By stepping out of that shame and committing to doing better, we will make progress. Fear of getting this wrong, and shame about past mistakes can stymie our progress. It often helps to remember that mistakes are an important part of learning. One of the dominant features of white culture is to internalize the false premise that nothing is worth doing unless we can do it perfectly. Focus on letting that notion go. Anti-racist transformation is messy.

So, close your eyes and let your mind go there, back to that time when you caught a biased thought in your own mind. Accept that you are human and these thoughts are part of being human. Now, summon the will to not only probe these memories for the insightful stories, but also to find a way to marshal these stories. Our small and great failures of character, nerve, or savvy reflect larger realities about the struggle to live alongside others and create one humanity within the universe. Our task this step and every step is to do work to see these connections, and to find a way to tell others so that they want to join us in the learning.

Goal

On steps 7 and 12, you took some notes on personal incidents related to unconscious bias and racial progress, respectively. If your thinking about these issues has evolved since those steps, you should add your reflections below. What directly follows is a brief overview of the structure of an anecdote and two illustrations.

Creating an Anecdote

A simple way of thinking about an anecdote is that it has three elements:

Setup: Context setting, with enough description of the physical, emotional, or social environment so that the listener can identify with you. If it is suitable, construct the setup so that it is not obvious what the key takeaway will be.

Key Moment: This is the heart of the story from an observation/experience perspective. It could be something that the central figure in the anecdote thought, something they observed, some action they took, or something that happened to them. Usually, the key moment is not the exact same thing as the takeaway (below), but they are closely related.

Takeaway: Not unlike the moral to a children's story, this is the overarching lesson, learning, or conclusion from the experience. Ideally, this is at least somewhat different from the key moment, but the lesson and the key moment should be constructed so that many if not most reasonable people would leave the experience with the same takeaway.

Here are two brief examples of anecdotes that allies have conveyed:

Anecdote #1 – on unconscious bias

Setup: I had heard about a food place that served chicken gizzards on the other side of town. I love gizzards, so I went to it. The place was in a mini-mart attached to a gas station on the black side of town. When I pulled up and parked, I noticed these two middle-aged guys drinking 40-ounce beers out of bags sitting near the door. They acknowledged me as I left my car and started to approach the door.

Key Moment: As this happened, my mind flashed on the idea that I needed to lock my doors, despite the fact that I could see the cook and the counter through the window and would never be out of sight of my car. There was even a police car in the parking lot! The cook was happy and surprised to see a white person coming for her food and we had a great conversation about the joy of gizzards. She named me "Gizzard Girl" that day and still calls me that when I come back.

Takeaway: The gap between the basic politeness of the guys with the beer and the niceness of the cook and my own completely unjustified fears of theft were very striking, and even embarrassing to me though no one but me knew what I thought. I guess certain prejudices are just deeply ingrained. And I have spent a lot of my career working in black communities!

Anecdote #2 – on racial progress

Setup: I grew up in northwest Indiana. I remember going to elementary school with a black boy named Kelsey (this was early 1980s). He was the only non-white student at my school, and his family was the only non-white family in the area. To me, he was like any other kid on the block, only with darker skin.

Key Moment: I later learned that he was harassed at school, his family's house and cars were vandalized, and a group from a nearby Baptist church burned a cross on their front lawn. They were forced to move out of the area due to threats of violence.

Takeaway: I do not think this would happen in that area today. If it did, it would be a big social media story. So, I guess this shows some progress.

Preparation

To construct your anecdote on unconscious bias, you should refer to your notes from step 7. If you have any additional reflections on your experiences with bias since you took those notes, write them here:

The most convincing anecdote will be one where you noticed yourself having a bias towards another person. If you don't have one of those, but have one or more bias stories in the other categories (you being a victim of bias or you witnessing bias operating between two other people) think through which of these would likely be most credible to a person who tends to believe unconscious bias does not exist.

In addition, if your thoughts about racial progress have evolved from step 12, make some notes about this also to strengthen your anecdote about racial progress:

Step 13 Tasks

Preparing Your Anecdote on Unconscious Bias

Setup: What are the key broad elements and specific details that help bring the listener to the situation?

Key moment: What is the moment when the bias became clear to you and would have to most people in the same situation?

Takeaway: What is the central idea about bias that stays with you from the experience?

Preparing Your Anecdotes About Racial Progress

Setup: What are the key broad elements and specific details that help bring the listener to the situation?

Key moment: What is the moment when notable racial progress became clear to you and would have to most people in the same situation?

Takeaway: What is the central idea about racial progress that stays with you from the experience?

Execution

- After you take some initial notes and refine them, practice your stories in the mirror.
- Do each of them at least twice, at different lengths.
    - One version should be less than one minute.
    - One version should take up 2-2.5 minutes without boring the listener.

Bonus Assignments

1. During the course of the next 24 hours, tell someone — preferably someone who IS NOT a skeptic — your unconscious bias story.
2. Tell someone your story about racial progress.
3. After relating your stories, ask them if they have any experiences that tend to affirm or disconfirm your takeaway from the story you told.

Reflections

What was your level of comfort telling your anecdotes?

Was your comfort level the same for each topic?

Did the duration you were focusing on affect your comfort level in telling your stories?

Are there any adjustments that you want to keep in mind as you think about telling these anecdotes in the wild?

Closing

"The key to the future of the world is finding optimistic stories and letting them be known." — Pete Seeger

Date / /

Step 14

Relaxing And Telling Your Stories

"We're so complex, we're mysteries to ourselves; we're difficult to each other. And then storytelling reminds us we're all the same." — Brad Pitt

Grounding — 3rd Principle:
Acceptance of one another and encouragement to spiritual growth in our congregations.

Step 14's Objective
- Experiment with a new relaxation method.
- Rehearse you Connect and Expand stories.

Every spiritual practice we engage in should bring some level of peace and relaxation. Whether it be yoga, knitting, or hiking in the woods; clearing the mind, paying attention to the mind-body connection, and feeling centered are some of the benefits. The practices help discipline the mind so that we can live our lives with greater intention to create a more loving world. Just as we engage in the search for radical love, we must simultaneously strive for radical forgiveness — for both ourselves and others. We are often much too hard on ourselves. It is often much easier to give accommodation and grace to other people than it is to ourselves.

Just as we must simultaneously hold onto the vision of a world that has progressed and one that is still far from perfect, we also must hold on to a vision of ourselves as having done much but with much more to do. Personal and spiritual transformation is about the journey much more than it is about the destination.

So, finding a way to come to a calm and holistic acceptance of the accomplishments we have made towards becoming our best selves helps us commit to connecting in love. Be brave enough to make a mistake. Even this acceptance of the complexity is only one half of the story; awareness of the need to keep pushing toward deeper understanding and personal growth is the countervailing force. As anti-racists, we can hold each other accountable and hold each other with love — simultaneously.

One way of working on our self-acceptance and our ability to hold these truths together is to further develop our ability to go to a place of relaxation and centeredness. Gaining better and quicker access to this place will help us not only accept our true nature, but also help us better connect to other people.

The primary goal this step is to begin experimenting with one-minute relaxation methods. A new one is being introduced to you. Now, you have five different methods to choose from throughout the course of this step. The suggestion is that you do the one-minute exercise once in the morning and just before the conversations that you will initiate.

Goal

To boost your growth in the toolkit methods the Boot Camp will emphasize the ways in which you interact with other people where disagreement will likely arise. In such cases, it is important to further refine your ability to get centered and stay centered. Practicing one-minute relaxation methods — which are short enough that you could excuse yourself and engage the method in a bathroom or private area just before the interaction you are preparing for — will be of great help.

In addition, you will continue ramping up toward using your racial progress and unconscious bias stories in the wild. You will practice telling them both in the mirror.

Part 1: Try a New Relaxation Method

Through the course of step 14, keep experimenting with the quick relaxation methods from the last few steps, except now do them for one minute instead of three. Of course, three minutes of relaxing is better than one, but people can get a noticeable benefit from focusing on getting centered and relaxed in just one minute.

It will be important to note how these techniques affect you when you give them less time.

1 minute Relaxation – Quick Stretch
- BREATHE IN—Reach up tall above your head.
- BREATHE OUT—Reach down low to the floor by your toes from the waist (just as far as is comfortable for you).
- BREATHE IN—Reach up to the sky again.
- BREATHE OUT—Return your hands to your side.
- Repeat 3-4 times.

Do the stretch routine now. Pay attention to how it affects your level of mind and body relaxation. Do one minute of one of your favorite relaxation methods that you have been experimenting with recently. Pay attention to its affect on you.

How would you assess the differential effect of these methods?

As you imagine trying to use them in a real situation (e.g. you see a difficult racial conversation coming, and briefly excuse yourself), what is your initial impression about the pros and cons of each method?

Try to practice at least one method twice. Take note of its effect on you.

Part 2: Practice Your Racial Progress Story, a Transition, and Unconscious Bias Story

In a few steps, you are going to tell your unconscious bias and racial progress stories to others and notice what effect the stories have on them and on you. This step, you will practice them in the mirror.

The first time you practice these methods, use the long version of the anecdote (suggested between 2 and 2.5 minutes). The second time, do the short version (suggested at about 45 seconds).

The sequence is below:
1. Say something aloud close to:
   "One thing not talked about enough is that I think there has been an improvement in racism over the decades."
2. Tell your racial progress story.
3. Say out loud something close to this:
   "Even though there has been improvement, I also think that racism is still an issue. In fact, sometimes I still see how racial bias is something that I see actively happening among people I know."

4. Then tell your unconscious bias story.
5. Close and synthesize the imaginary conversation like this:
   "Maybe it's possible that both things are true. Racism is better than it used to be and is also still a problem that we should think about."

Reflections

How did it feel to tell the stories? Was your comfort level related to the subject or the duration of the story?

Any other takeaways from the exercise this step?

Closing

"There are no secrets to success. It is the result of preparation, hard work, and learning from failure."
— Colin Powell

Step 15

Reflection And Synthesis

"Zen masters say you cannot see your reflection in running water, only in still water." — Elizabeth Gilbert

Grounding — 1st Stone:
Religious liberalism depends on the principle that revelation is continuous. Our tradition is a living tradition because we are always learning new truths.

Step 15's Objective
- Create written answers in response to reflection questions.

You are halfway through this Boot Camp. Whether you are doing this day-by-day as an intensive experience, or at another frequency in a small group or alone, you have covered half of the material. This step will pause and reflect on your recent progress. Being an ally is tiring work, so it is in everyone's best interest for you to take measures to sustain and expand your capacity for this work. That is why this book is written as a spiritual practice guide. Inspirational quotes and reading for the beginning and ending of each assignment, a framing in Universalist values, and deeper connection to progressive ideas are all provided so that you nurture your spirit. Be sure to check in on how your spirit is feeling.

The specific reflection assignment focuses on the analysis of the new skills you are learning about conversations about race and racism. It is perfectly acceptable for your reflection to also include other issues and questions, such as those related to your own spiritual practices relevant to this work. How are you able to manage your reaction to people you disagree with? Are you seeing people you disagree with differently? Perhaps with more humanity?

Other things to reflect on: Do you engage the tasks more thoroughly when you do your meditation the night before, in the morning, or some other time? Have you found any additional spiritual rituals, such as a moment of prayer or silence, that tend to augment your engagement with this material? Does talking to other people about what you are doing tend to stoke your focus or to dissipate it? Are you using a touchstone to remind yourself why you are bothering to do this work? There are many ways to engage spiritually. The important thing to remember is that what works for you is the thing you should engage in. What doesn't feed your spirit should be left by the wayside. You are becoming a Compassionate Warrior.

Reflections

Every seven Boot Camp steps, it is useful to review and assess progress. The path toward increased competency includes frequent pauses to reflect, assess, and make needed adjustments. The central

question is: **What were your top takeaways from the past seven steps of Boot Camp activities?** One way to get at that question is to specifically reflect upon each of the skills you have been working on.
Over the past several Boot Camp steps, what are your lessons learned and reflections?

Your relaxation practices?

Your listening inclinations and skills?

Your relationships with racism skeptics?

Your ability/willingness to search for agreement with those whose views you disagree with?

Your confidence in your storytelling?

Your perspective on unconscious bias?

Your perspective on racial progress?

Are there notable insights that you want to keep in mind as your progress continues?

Closing

"When we love, we always strive to become better than we are. When we strive to become better than we are, everything around us becomes better too." — Paulo Coelho

Date / /

Step 16

Listening Attentively

"The greatest gift you can give another is the purity of your attention."
— Richard Moss

Grounding — 5th Principle:
The right of conscience and the use of the democratic process within our congregations and in society at large. The goal of world community, with peace, liberty and justice for all.

Step 16's Objectives
- Begin experimenting with a new type of Listening Tip.
- Use that Listening Tip after asking someone to answer a question about their views of racism.

Democratic principles are fundamentally grounded in the idea that all voices in society count and need to be taken seriously. In reality, democracy allows the tyranny of the majority. Our constitutional amendments and balance of power in government were meant to be attempts to mitigate that unbridled power. The compromises that lead to the original Constitution and Bill of Rights were hammered out through debates, arguments, and private discussions where dramatically opposing viewpoints were allowed time to be heard. In our modern society, opportunities for dialogue between people with differing opinions is often avoided. This is the problem this Boot Camp is addressing: readiness for engagement in those unpleasant, yet deeply rich conversations that move the needle on progress.

Additionally, as we grow as allies, we commit ourselves to working for goals that might not directly benefit us. We also commit to learning more and more about the systems that perpetuate bondage, inequity, and injustice. In order to be change agents we resist the temptation to try to solve things systematically until we have done the spade work for change in our own personal circles. We stay committed to bringing our own community together, increasing their capacity for making change. We can do this by making a strong commitment to developing our own listening skills, which will build peace in our own families and neighborhoods by making attentive listening a part of our everyday practice.

Being a force for more listening is an important way of showing the people in our circle that we care about them and that they matter. Increasing listening in our communities will help heal some of the divides. Having a practice of listening also expands our spirit, in that a developed habit of deep listening can help keep us from the self-absorption and self-centeredness our culture tries to imbue in us. Listening is a generous act. Generosity begets generosity, including the generosity of spirit involved in deep listening.

By personally being a force for listening, we help move the culture of our family, our congregations, and society in general just by embodying the ethos of listening and advancing democracy by focusing on its intent to include all voices.

Goal

This step you will experiment with a new type of Listening Tip. You will also use the tip in a conversation about racism with someone who is NOT likely to disagree with you about it.

The following list of Listening Tips, potentially useful both before and during a difficult conversation, focus on how you can improve your listening by managing your own background thoughts.

1. Remind yourself that just because you listen empathetically to a point of view does not mean that you agree with it.
2. Tell yourself to listen for experiences that may be similar to ones you have had.
3. Consciously listen for potential openings for future conversations.
4. Remind yourself to listen for the underlying needs that are behind statements you hear.
5. Notice things that make the two of you similar to each other as well as things that you can agree on.

Choose two techniques you think have the best chance of working for you. If there are some other techniques that work better for you, include them.

List which ones you have chosen:

Assignment

This step, you will ask a white person about their views on whether they think that racism against people of color is a specific problem that needs specific attention or whether they think racism against all people is equally important. It is best if you choose someone who you think or know would agree with you that racism against POC is a more serious problem. Put differently, your goal is to choose someone you have strong reason to believe is an ally, the way that this workbook has been using that term.

Your goal is to have them express their answer, then to ask them for a personal experience related to how they see it. Sometime during this encounter, you will engage one of the Listening Tips. Your goal is also to listen to them in a way that makes them feel heard.

If this feels uncomfortable and you want to tell them that you are in process of developing your listening skills, do that. But you will have a better test of your conversational skills if you do not reveal this. If possible, do not reveal that you are working on a skill—try to approach this as a natural conversation you initiated out of curiosity.

If they ask you for your perspective on the issue, tell them that you will get back to them at another time, because you want to really think about what they said. If they seem uncomfortable or insist, just answer the question naturally, perhaps using your story about witnessing unconscious bias. If possible, though, try to end the conversation with your attention on their story and your having expressed some gratitude for their sharing it.

If you wind up telling your unconscious bias story, note that it will function as a Connect story, since you and the person agree racism remains a problem. In the upcoming steps, we will return to the way that a racial progress story will likely be a Connect story for a skeptic and an Expand story for an ally. Similarly, your unconscious bias story will be an Expand story for a skeptic and a Connect story for an ally.

If the person is a skeptic AND insists that you tell them your perspective, tell them your story about how you feel racism has diminished over time.

Write down two possibilities for whom you might engage on this topic this step:

Assessment

As soon as you can after the encounter, answer the following questions:

1. How smooth or awkward was your question about their beliefs?

   ☐ Very Smooth | ☐ Smooth | ☐ Kinda Smooth/Kinda Clunky | ☐ Clunky | ☐ Very Clunky

2. How smooth was your question that transitioned them from belief to experience?

   ☐ Very Smooth | ☐ Smooth | ☐ Kinda Smooth/Kinda Clunky | ☐ Clunky | ☐ Very Clunky

3. How well do you think you listened?

   ☐ Very Well | ☐ Pretty Well | ☐ OK | ☐ Not Great | ☐ Pretty Poorly

4. How much do you think they felt heard? They:

   ☐ Felt very heard | ☐ Felt heard | ☐ Felt kind of heard | ☐ Did not feel heard

Reflections

1. How did it feel to approach a conversation(s) with a focus on listening?

2. How did the experience of engaging people in this way compared to what you expected?

3. Who was the person and what were the circumstances?

4. Which Listening Tip did you use and how/when did you use it?

5. How smooth/awkward were your opening question and your experience question?

6. How well did you listen? What were the driving forces behind how well you did?

Note: On Boot Camp Step 28 the task will be to have an Apologetic Non-Apology encounter — preferably with a skeptic in your circle. Think about whether you need to start engineering this encounter, even if you only interact with this person infrequently. If so, this may be a good time to start reaching out to them to reawaken your communication channel. This will make your doing the ANA seem less out of place.

Also, on Boot Camp Step 24, your task will involve an encounter with your Boot Camp buddy. If you need to give them the heads up about engaging them at that time, do so.

Closing

"If there is to be peace in the world,
There must be peace in the nations.
If there is to be peace in the nations,
There must be peace in the cities.
If there is to be peace in the cities,
There must be peace between neighbors.
If there is to be peace between neighbors,
There must be peace in the home.
If there is to be peace in the home,
There must be peace in the heart." — Lao-Tse

Step 17

Asking For The Experience Of A Skeptic

"The greatest compliment that was ever paid me was when one asked me what I thought, and attended to my answer." —Henry David Thoreau

Grounding — 5th Principle:
The right of conscience and the use of the democratic process within our congregations and in society at large.

Step 17's Objective
- Practice an Ask with someone likely to have a view about racism that you disagree with.

This step we get to the hardest part - actually engaging a racism skeptic. Before we begin, let's explore the term "The right of conscience." It is a term that has many meanings and has been invoked in a wide variety of contexts, from Catholic Church Doctrine to health care legislation. The reason we center the right to conscience this step is because we are going to try to compassionately take on someone who has the right to a different viewpoint through the power of listening, not arguing; hopefully, we can move them a millimeter toward allyship.

One of the hardest concepts we grapple with as people of faith is the question, when is someone no longer worthy of respect or dignity? This can certainly be true as we strategize about whom to engage. We ask ourselves: Who can possibly be converted from skeptic to ally? The foundations of Christianity include the many parables of Jesus keeping company with whores and lepers. In progressive faith traditions, we often easily see the parallel in not condemning people to death, but we can easily be consumed with disdain and lack of empathy for folks on the other side of the political spectrum. We are especially intolerant of racism skeptics; therefore, we must consciously grant "The right of conscience" to people with whom we disagree — even on the topic of race and racism.

We must embrace the idea that each person has the right to their own thoughts and perspectives about the world and about their own experience. In addition, "the right of conscience" is intended to remind us that others have the same level of regard and attachment to their points of view as each of us have to ours. Take a breath. Let go of your judgment. Get curious.

Asking For the Experience of a Skeptic
One might summarize the perspective we need to adopt in this quote: "We walk the same earth, but have come to vastly different conclusions that I struggle to respect...please share with me what happened to lead you to think like you do." If we truly believe in the right of conscience of each person, a curiosity about the experiences that formed that conscience emerges almost naturally.

This step is the first where, having augmented your compassion tools of Listening Tips and skills in asking experience questions, you are going to purposely engage in a conversation with someone who likely disagrees with you about racism.

Background

You have already practiced your relaxation method, asking about experience, attentively listening, and not expressing your perspective. This step, the goal is to do that with someone you predict will have rather different views of racial issues than you.

Preparation

- Think about whom you will engage and how you might create the best atmosphere for the encounter— for yourself and for them.
- Plan to do the one-minute relaxation method just before your conversation.
- Choose a Listening Tip. Pick one you think would be most effective in this situation.
- If it would make you more relaxed, give them the heads up that you are doing this as part of an effort to work on your listening.
- If you do this, it may be helpful to mention that you have been engaging many people with many different viewpoints. If possible, just approach this as a natural conversation.
- If possible, choose someone with whom you HAVE NOT had a difficult race conversation in the past.

Execution

1. Tell them you would like to have a short conversation about something that you have been thinking about.
2. Ask them if they think that racism has changed enough so that it equally affects all groups or whether it still affects traditionally disadvantaged groups more than others.
3. After they answer the question, ask them for a recent or formative experience that shapes their view. At some point, paraphrase what they said to confirm that you understood it.
4. Thank them for sharing their experience.

Note: As before, if they try to draw your views out, tell them that you will get back to them at a later point. If demurring on the question would make your relationship awkward, tell them that you think that racism has declined, and tell them your racial progress story. If you do this, get out of the conversation while signaling that there is more to discuss later, and you may want to come back to this topic.

Assessment

As soon as possible after the conversation, make some mental or written notes about:
- The questions you used to spark the conversation
- How well you listened
- The effectiveness of the relaxation techniques and the Listening Tips
- How well you closed the conversation
- How the process felt

Reflections

Who was the person and what were the circumstances?

Which Listening Tip did you use and how/when did you use it?

How smooth/awkward were your opening question and your experience question? What could have been better, if anything?

☐ Very Smooth | ☐ Smooth | ☐ Kinda Smooth/Kinda Clunky | ☐ Clunky | ☐ Very Clunky

How well did you listen? What were the driving forces behind how well you did?

☐ Very well | ☐ Well | ☐ OK | ☐ Not great | ☐ Poorly

How did the entire interaction make you feel? What are your takeaways from the experience?

Closing

When death comes like the hungry bear in autumn;
when death comes and takes all the bright coins from his purse
to buy me, and snaps the purse shut;
when death comes
like the measle-pox
when death comes
like an iceberg between the shoulder blades,
I want to step through the door full of curiosity
— Excerpt from *When Death Comes* by Mary Oliver

Date / /

Step 18

Preparing An Apologetic Non-Apology For Two Skeptics

"Apologizing does not always mean you're wrong and the other person is right. It just means you value your relationship more than your ego."
— *Mark Matthews*

Grounding — 7th Principle: Respect for the interdependent web of all existence of which we are a part.

Step 18's Objective
- Prepare the ANA for two racism skeptics in your circle.

As a people of covenantal faith, our religion expresses itself and exists between and among us, not as separate scripture or doctrine that is constant or tangible. Our faith flows through, between, and around us. Each time we encounter one another, learn something new, or move forward, we have changed it and it has changed us. Rifts in our relationships disrupt our equilibrium and throw us off our center, even if only in subtle ways, so being in right relations with as many people as possible is essential for our well-being, and it will make the world a better place. It is in our personal interest to create harmony in our relationships, if only because this external harmony helps our struggle to maintain inner peace.

When someone else has been the primary cause of a rift in our relationship, we are just as responsible to heal it as when we are the cause. Even when the other person, in our opinion, caused the rift, we probably did or thought something that helped contribute to the disconnection. The good news is that we have the power to reset relationships on our own. Even if both people contributed to harming a relationship, one person can start the process of rebuilding it. To err is human, to love without expecting anything in return, is divine.

Before the end of the Boot Camp, you will have attempted to reset your communication with someone with whom you have previously had a difficult conversation about race. This step you will prepare an Apologetic Non-Apology for two different racism skeptics.

Background
Your goal is to think about two people who are racism skeptics with whom you have had at least a somewhat unpleasant moment in a conversation about race. Hopefully, you have reasonable access to them— even if only by telephone—but in person is much, much better. Before the Boot Camp ends, you will actually use the ANA in a conversation with at least one of them.

Preparation

Name of Skeptic #1:

Where and when was the difficult conversation about race, and what was the topic?

What did you think or do that was unhelpful to your connection?

How could you describe what you did in a way that is honest but not off-putting?

As you imagine talking to them about this, how do you think you will feel?

What is an honest statement you can make about not doing this again?

How would you phrase an experience question if you wanted to open the topic again?

Name of Skeptic #2:

Where and when was the difficult conversation about race, and what was the topic?

What did you think or do that was unhelpful to your connection?

How could you describe what you did in a way that is honest but not off-putting?

As you imagine talking to them about this, how do you think you will feel?

What is an honest statement you can make about not doing this again?

How would you phrase an experience question if you wanted to open the topic again?

Execution

After you have completed the questions above, imagine you are about to have a conversation with Skeptic #1, practice one of the one-minute revelation methods, then say the Apologetic Non-Apology to the mirror. Reflect a bit on how it went, do a relaxation exercise to reset yourself, and then repeat the exercise for Skeptic #2.

As a reminder, this is the form of the Apologetic Non-Apology:

1. Recall the prior conversation and what you did or thought that was unhelpful to connectedness.
2. Say how you are feeling right now.
3. Commit to not repeating the mistake; confirm that it's okay to ask experience questions on the topic

Here is an example:

- "A few months back we were talking about poverty, and I was recalling that conversation recently. I realized that during that conversation **I talked over you a lot**. I have to admit that I am **somewhat nervous** just bringing this up now. I want to say that **I don't plan to do that** in the future, and I want to say that if we ever talk about that topic again, **I will try to ask you about what you have seen** that makes you see the situation as you do."

Reflections

What was your emotional reaction as you answered the preparation question? Was it different for the two skeptics?

How did it feel to practice the ANA in the mirror? Was there a difference in how the mirror practice exercise felt with respect to the two skeptics?

How easy or difficult is it to imagine actually doing the ANA with these people?

Any other reflections about the exercise?

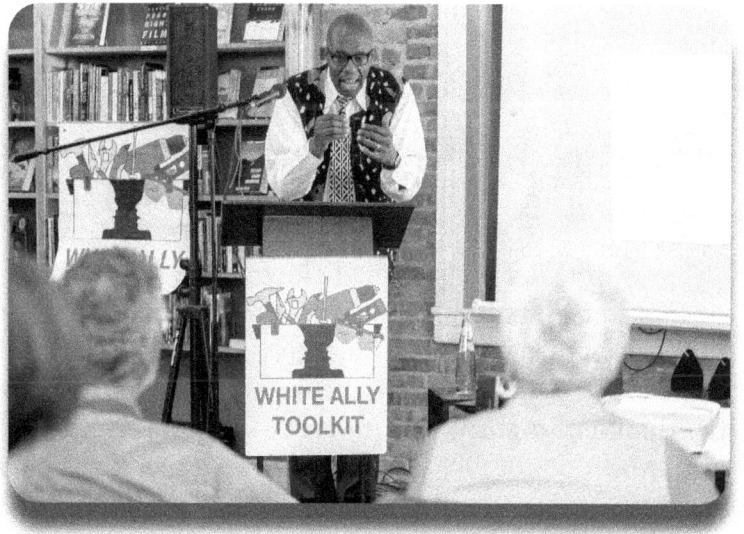

Closing

We arrive out of many singular rooms, walking over the branching streets.
We come to be assured that brothers and sisters surround us, to restore their images on our eyes.
We enlarge our voices in common speaking and singing.
— Excerpt from *We Arrive Out of Many Singular Rooms*, Hymn #443: Singing the Living Tradition

Date / /

Step 19

Finding Ideas You Agree With Embedded Within Racially Problematic Statements

"Diplomacy is listening to what the other guy needs. Preserving your own position, but listening to the other guy. You have to develop relationships with other people so when the tough times come, you can work together."
—*Colin Powell*

Grounding — 1st Principle:
The inherent worth and dignity of every person. A free and responsible search for truth and meaning.

Step 19's Objective
- Find ideas you can agree with that are embedded within racially problematic statements you disagree with.

As spiritual people, we believe everyone has inherent worth and deserves to be treated with dignity. As a practical matter, keeping this idea at the top of one's mind is difficult, especially when others reflect racist or other views that inherently deny the worth and dignity of other people. To make matters more difficult, there are massive media organizations polluting our society and promoting views that fuel the denial of dignity. It is natural to respond to this information with resistance and avoidance and to minimize our contact with fans of these messages because they can be toxic to us and are toxic to our society.

Yet, the higher spiritual path is not to turn away in disgust from perspectives that are anathema to us. The higher spiritual path is to presume that the people who hold these views are not worthless people and are not people who are fundamentally separate from ourselves. They are part of our shared humanity, live in our neighborhoods, and often are part of our own families. Therefore, it is our challenge to try to find a point of commonality within views we disagree with, and do so in the service of supporting and growing a genuine connection with someone we deeply disagree with in order to combat the toxicity with love, respect, dignity, and equanimity.

Reminding ourselves of the worth and dignity of each person can help us find common ground with them, reminding them that we, too, are worthy of dignity and respect. As we commit to helping skeptics engage with information that is contrary to their beliefs, keep in mind that they are also on a journey, seeking truth and meaning in their own lives, and your conversations with them are meant to plant seeds of understanding, acceptance, and progress toward racial equity.

As you ramp up to engage skeptics, it is valuable to practice the skill of what was previously called "finding the chocolate in the trail mix." This step's task builds on the work that you did on step 6, when you took in news stories from a perspective that you disagree with.

To further develop your ability to do this when people say things when you don't expect, you will practice on racially problematic statements that you hear now and then.

Assignment

On step 1, you wrote down several racially problematic statements that you sometimes hear and that bother you. The core task this step is to review those statements and think about ideas embedded within them that you might be able to agree with.

Return to Step 1: Review your notes on skeptics you spoke with and their statements that bothered you.

Step 1: Review and re-copy your racially problematic statements from step 1 below. If this statement came from a specific skeptic in your circle, make a note of that. At first, don't worry about writing down the "but I do agree" statements. We will come back to that.

1. I don't agree with this the idea that: *(rewrite a condensed version of Statement 1 below)*

    but I do agree that:

2. I don't agree with the idea that: *(rewrite a condensed version of Statement 2 below)*

    but I do agree that:

3. I don't agree with the idea that: *(rewrite a condensed version of Statement 3 below)*

    but I do agree that:

4. I don't agree with idea that: *(rewrite a condensed version of Statement 4 below)*

    but I do agree that:

Your goal is to find an appropriate rejoinder to a racially problematic statement. Find one that you actually believe and that a skeptic would likely agree with. Two examples of appropriate rejoinders are:

Example 1	Example 2
I don't believe in the idea that:	I don't believe in the idea that:
Very few people are racist any more.	*Every group gets treated fairly by law enforcement.*
But I do agree that:	But I do agree that:
Racism has diminished a lot.	*There are many good cops on the street.*

Notice that your existing racial progress story is appropriate for Example 1. Also notice that the racial progress story would only be a marginally appropriate rejoinder for the second statement about police mistreatment. The rejoinder provided above is much more targeted to the actual statement.

Of the statements that you wrote down, make an assessment of how well your racial progress story would act as an appropriate rejoinder.

The goal of the exercise is to clarify rejoinder statements for at least two of the racially problematic statements that you took note of on step 1. It will be a useful mental exercise to think about rejoinders for all four statements.

- Once you have identified rejoinders for at least two of the statements, think about which statements seem most suitable for you to create an anecdote around. Make some notes about which rejoinders you think would provide the most fertile ground for a personal anecdote that you could create.
  - *You will come back to these notes during the last two steps of the Boot Camp.*
- Look at the statements to see if your existing Connect and Expand stories might be appropriate responses to the statement by the skeptics if they were to express such sentiments again.
- Make a note of which skeptics you now have a road map for a conversation after the Boot Camp is over.
- If the statement does not map well onto your existing stories, review the list of statements you made for what you believe. For each one, explore how easy it might be to create a story of a formative or recent experience that animates what you do believe.
- Put an asterisk by the two statements that it would be easiest to form a story around.
  - *You will come back to this on the last step of Boot Camp, when you will chart future activities that you will take beyond this Boot Camp.*

Bonus Assignment

Find another person who you think is likely to be an ally and repeat the exercise from step 18. As was the case on step 18, vary the order in which you deliver your stories depending on how they answer your inquiry about their perspective.

Note: on step 29, the task is to create an ANA encounter, preferably with one of your skeptics. If you need to take special measures so that you can have an encounter with this person, it may be useful to start taking those steps.

Reflections

How did you feel about looking for something you could agree with that was embedded within the racially problematic statements? If there was a part of you that wanted to avoid the exercise, what are the lessons learned from noticing this part of you?

Look back at which statements you "found the chocolate" for. Focus on the embedded ideas you jotted down. Try to think of the core subject of a personal story that illustrates your belief in the idea. Make a short note to yourself about the memory from which you might be able to build an anecdote.

Are there any skeptics in your circle who have made problematic statements that you may have a rejoinder for? If so, you may be able to create a strategy for talking to those skeptics, based on further developing a Connect story they can agree with and an Expand story that will subsequently invite them to think differently.

Closing

"I was a victim of a stereotype. There were only two of us Negro kids in the whole class, and our English teacher was always stressing the importance of rhythm in poetry. Well, everybody knows — except us — that all Negroes have rhythms, so they elected me class poet."
— Langston Hughes

Date / /

Step 20

Tell Your Stories To An Ally

"The story—from Rumpelstiltskin to War and Peace—is one of the basic tools invented by the human mind for the purpose of understanding. There have been great societies that did not use the wheel, but there have been no societies that did not tell stories. — Ursula K. Le Guin

Grounding — 5th Smooth Stone:
Liberalism holds that the resources (divine and human) that are available for the achievement of meaningful change justify an attitude of ultimate optimism.

Step 20's Objectives
- Initiate a conversation about race with someone you predict is an ally.
- Follow the RACE method, including telling your racial progress and unconscious bias stories.

As we strive to create a better world, we will stay energized if we presume that there are more than enough building blocks available to world changers, if we only can figure out how to marshal them. Our own stories are a part of that. Even if it felt like a struggle to find stories from our past that might help you expand your toolkit, the opportunity here is to reconnect to that optimism that the solution to almost any problem in front of you is already within you.

Background

You will come across as more natural in encounters with skeptics if you are not relying on the same anecdotes all the time. Thus, it is important to expand your toolkit and create some additional anecdotes that you can deploy in the right moment. The goal of this step is to develop an additional Connect story and to practice it in the mirror.

Before the end of the Boot Camp, you will have two Expand stories (most likely both about unconscious bias, although one may be about white privilege) and two Connect stories, one about racial progress and one about unabashed bigotry in someone you have known.

Many people in the anti-racism community use labels like "white supremacy culture" or "the patriarchy" to refer to a wide swath of people who have low racial literacy or racially unsophisticated views. This kind of language and perspective has a value within internal conversations among people fighting racism and helps anti-racists see the complex interrelationships between different ways that racism manifests itself. In this view, there is an important connection between hardcore white supremacist organizers, people who feel a good deal of racial resentment but would probably never attend a white supremacist rally, and other folks with less overtly problematic views. This perspective usually also sees people with explicitly anti-racist views, but who still have residual racial bias (e.g. you), as connected and part of the same continuum.

What is at issue is when is it useful to focus on the connection between these perspectives, and when is it useful to not focus on the connection. In a conversation with a skeptic who has been trained to dismiss almost all analysis of systemic racism, it is valuable to make a distinction between different points on this continuum — at least at first. The perspective that all these views are part of white supremacy culture feels to a skeptic like they are being inappropriately linked to people they abhor. Many people who proudly claim to "not see color" have, in fact, done some active resisting of racist messages from others to come to their current views on racial issues, even if many allies see them as not sufficiently evolved and would judge their racial literacy as relatively low.

Your goal in calling to mind a bigot you have known is to convey that you make a moral distinction between the views of people who are virulently racist and the ones that you and the skeptic hold. Later, when you tell your unconscious bias story, you will convey that while those moral distinctions hold, you can see a connection between the thoughts you sometimes have and the noxious thoughts that bigots are consumed by all the time. But during the Connect story, your objective is to put distance between the perspective of a bigot you have known and the more racially open perspective of you and the skeptic.

Execution

Part 1: Search your memory for potential incidents to focus on.

Provided are some questions to probe your memory. Jot down a few notes about your experiences that relate to any of these questions.

- Can you think of a person (adult or another child) who tried to get you to accept their racially bigoted views when you were growing up? What did they do? How did you respond to their efforts to pull you into their views?
- As an adult, have you come across someone who you would say has views that are so racist that hearing them troubles you? How did these views come out? What did you do?
- Are there any people in your circle of contacts (whom you see at least once every couple of years, say) who hold views about race that make you feel uncomfortable? What are some things they

Connect Story Example: "The Real Bigot is Over There."
- *The following paraphrases the story that an ally told during a workshop.*
- **Setup:** I have a grandfather who has always tried to get us to buy into his bigoted views. When I was a child, he would tell us to not play with the one or two kids of color in my neighborhood. He even told me that their dirty skin would rub off on my siblings and me if we played with them. One time when he learned about my sister dating someone when she was 15 years old, his response was, "That is a little young to be dating, but as long as the guy is not black, I can live with it."
- **Key Moment:** Now he knows that he can't persuade us about his views and doesn't really try. But at any family gathering when the news comes on, we know we will hear comments on news stories like, "those folks just don't like to work," or "I think all of these complaints about police brutality are attempts to weaken law enforcement." It is really irritating to be around him and hear this. Now, we mostly just tune him out.
- **Takeaway:** I am really glad that neither my grandfather nor any other racist adults influenced me like this, aren't you? That perspective is really unhealthy for society.

have said that make you feel that way? What do you do when these situations come up?

- Are there any other examples that you can think of that don't fit these questions but that illustrate you having a personal encounter with a white person with racially troublesome views? *(Do not count seeing someone in mass or social media who had bigoted views; however, if you have had an exchange on social media with someone like this, that might be suitable.)*

Part 2: Choose an incident, expand it into an anecdote

After letting your mind percolate on these questions for a few minutes and jotting some notes, choose one of these incidents and create an anecdote about it. You will use the same structure as before, with a set-up, a key moment, and a takeaway.

- What is the setup?
- What is the key moment?
- What is the takeway?

Part 3: Mirror Practice

After you have developed your anecdotes, practice them in the mirror.

Reflections

Which relaxation method did you use? How well did it work?

Which Listening Tip did you use? How well did it work?

How would you rate your success in making the person feel heard? They:
☐ Felt very heard | ☐ Felt heard | ☐ Felt kinda heard | ☐ Did not feel heard

How smooth was your questioning about their point of view and experience? Why?
☐ Very Smooth | ☐ Smooth | ☐ Kinda Smooth/Kinda Clunky | ☐ Clunky | ☐ Very Clunky

How smooth was your transition to your Connect story, and how well did you tell it? Why?
☐ Very Smooth | ☐ Smooth | ☐ Kinda Smooth/Kinda Clunky | ☐ Clunky | ☐ Very Clunky

How smooth was your transition to your Expand story, and how well did you tell it? Why?
☐ Very Smooth | ☐ Smooth | ☐ Kinda Smooth/Kinda Clunky | ☐ Clunky | ☐ Very Clunky

How did your close the encounter?

What are your takeaways from this experience?

Closing
"The human mind is a story processor, not a logic processor."
— Jonathan Haidt

Date / /

Step 21

Develop A Second Unconscious Bias Story

"There's always room for a story that can transport people to another place." — J.K. Rowling

Grounding — Stone 1: Religious Liberalism depends on the principle that "revelation" is continuous. Our religious tradition is a living tradition because we are always learning new truths.

Step 21's Objective
* Begin working on two additional stories: one about racial progress and one about unconscious bias

It is hard to accept the fact that even very good-hearted people are not immune to the widespread idea that some people are more deserving than others. But we cannot be afraid to look at ourselves honestly, including looking at the relatively dark places in our minds or hearts that reflect neither most of our nature nor our higher ambitions.

But look we must do, especially if we are trying to get others to take an honest measure of themselves. We must show leadership in this ourselves, first by having the humility to fearlessly look inward, then having the courage to share what we find.

Finding and telling others about the places within us that need the most work is actually doing the work of making these places smaller.

Goal

As noted on step 20, your objective is to build your arsenal of stories so that you are not relying on the same anecdotes all the time. Over the course of your life, your bank of stories should grow and grow. For this Boot Camp, the goal is to finish the process with at least two Expand and two Connect stories.

This step's task is to develop a 2nd story that illustrates your thoughts being affected by an unconscious racial bias. If you absolutely cannot find a second example, you can follow the instructions to find a story about unearned racial advantage, which is usually called white privilege. Here is why we suggest you prioritize a second unconscious bias story over a story about privilege.

Over the course of your allyship, having compelling stories about the ways that you benefit from privilege is essential to being persuasive. However, a story about advantages that you experience because you are white is almost always more complex and involves more extrapolation than stories about unconscious bias. Privilege stories almost always involve some implicit comparison of the actual world with an alternative perspective of a person of color or even an alternative set of circumstances. In addition, concluding that white privilege matters will often bump up against a skeptic's attachment to the deeply ingrained ideas about merit.

By contrast, bias stories involve you noticing how your own mind is operating. There is less speculation involved in imagining how your mind might work if bias were not involved. Furthermore, every person knows that they sometimes have thoughts they are in control over, and perhaps not proud of. It might be easier for a skeptic to admit to themselves that they have racially problematic thoughts than that they have benefited from being white.

At the end of content for this step, there will be some bonus content for those who want to work on a privilege story. If you want to use this Boot Camp step to develop both a 2nd bias story and a privilege story, feel free. The more stories in your arsenal, the more flexibly you can respond to different situations.

Assignment

Part 1: Preparing your second story on unconscious bias

Review your notes from step 7. Look for experiences that might be the basis of a second anecdote about racial bias different than the one you already have.

Part 2: Choose an incident, expand it into an anecdote

After assessing the experiences that come to mind, focus on one of them and turn the incident into an anecdote with a structure that will help you keep the key points in mind whether you are telling the short or long version of the anecdote.

- What is the set up?
- What is the key moment?
- What is the takeaway?

Part 3: Mirror Practice

After you have developed your anecdotes, practice them in the mirror.

Bonus Content: Developing an Unearned Racial Advantage/White Privilege Story

Generally, the ACT project does not use the term "white privilege" to signify the many ways that being white is an advantage in modern America. As one workshop participant said, "Both the 'white' and the 'privilege' seem to trigger people." Instead, the project typically uses the term "unearned racial advantage." The reader can note that 1) this term is more descriptive, 2) a person from any group can experience this, even though the impact and breadth of advantage will vary, 3) the absence of the word "privilege" removes the association with class privilege, which is often a distraction in conversations.

Literature about race and racism is full of material about white privilege, so this is a topic that is easy to find information about; most people committed to anti-racism enough to engage this document have already become familiar with the key ideas. Thus, following is not meant as a full tutorial, and is merely one way of thinking about it that may prompt searches of your memory so you access your personal stories about it.

One way of thinking about unearned racial advantage is to divide it into a few somewhat distinct categories, such as:

Spared Injustice

Being less subject to racial discrimination has two direct benefits. First, some people experience little or no harmful discrimination. Second, people in the advantaged group experience much less of a drag on their daily psyche because of worries that they might experience disparate treatment. The domains of this lessened real and anticipated discrimination include virtually every area of life: education, health care, interactions with police, shopping, applications for life-changing opportunities like employment, housing, and loans, and so on. In a wide variety of areas, research has demonstrated that the concerns that whites are shielded from are not imagined, and that there are real disparities in how people of color are treated compared to whites.

Unspoken Whiteness

In many ways, white is the default in American society, and this shows up in number of ways, with different levels of significance.

- "Nude" bandages, pantyhose and similar objects usually mean "relative to white skin"
- Lead characters in media artifacts (TV shows, movies, news) are typically white
- Institutional leaders are typically white

Unjust Enrichment

The overt discrimination by institutions in prior historical periods has produced vast disparities in wealth compared to other groups that tend to accumulate over the generations. Some examples of this wealth include:

- White soldiers accessing the GI Bill
- White families benefiting from restrictive covenants, redlining, and FHA loans
- Professions allowing middle-class incomes excluding participation by non-whites
- Legacy admissions policies that perpetuate advantages from previous eras

Assignment

Search your memories and jot down notes on whichever of the following comes to your mind:

1. Can you think of a situation in which you benefited from white privilege because you were spared an injustice or were spared from worrying about an injustice? What are the feelings that you had at the time or have in retrospect about this experience?

2. Can you think of a situation where you benefited from white privilege because of the way that whiteness is the default? What thoughts or feelings did you have in the moment or in retrospect?

3. Can you think of a situation where you benefited from white privilege because racism in the past allowed important experiences or resources to be accrued to you? What were your thoughts or feelings when you first discovered that this was the case?

4. Can you think of a situation when you benefited from white privilege simply because you were in the group with larger numbers of people and were not in the minority?

After you jot down some notes about situations relevant to these questions, pick one to create an anecdote around.

- What is the set-up?

- What is the key moment?

- What is the takeaway?

After you have developed your anecdote, practice it in the mirror.

Closing

"God made man because he loves stories." — Elie Wiesel

Date / /

Step 22

Reflection And Synthesis

"It's on the strength of observation and reflection that one finds a way. So we must dig and delve unceasingly." — Claude Monet

Grounding — 4th Principle: A free and responsible search for truth and meaning.

Step 22's Objective
*   Create written answers in response to reflection questions.

As people of liberal, progressive faith, we embrace the process of becoming. In learning and doing, we change both ourselves and the people and places around us.

We acknowledge with gratitude that there are times in life when important insight, revelation, and awe emerge from within us with almost no effort. As realists, we also acknowledge that sometimes our epiphanies come because we focus our minds and concentration on making sense of our lives.

This step is the last step of the Boot Camp to be set aside exclusively for reflection and integration of recent lessons. By engaging this process of reflection actively, we add some kindling to our unconscious mind that is always burning for higher wisdom. Our decision to energetically and courageously search for the insights that might not be instantly apparent is a vital part of being caring stewards of our own growth and the betterment of the world.

You have practiced the RACE method and begun to expand your Toolkit even further. Before you push your skill set out even more, it is useful to take stock.

Reflections

Over the past Boot Camp steps, what are your lessons learned and reflections about:
Your relaxation practices?

Your skill in asking questions that transition from beliefs to experience?

Your listening inclinations and skills?

Your relationships with racism skeptics?

Your ability/willingness to search for agreement with those whose views you disagree with?

Your confidence in your story telling? How has it changed over the past Boot Camp steps?

What have your learned about how to be more effective?

Your perspective on unconscious bias?

Your goal this step is to get some practice in telling your second Connect and Expand stories to someone who you anticipate looks at racism similarly to the way you do.

Assignment

Your skills in storytelling in the service of allyship will always be growing. In addition, there will always be the first time you tell your story in service of wielding influence. This step, you will use your second set of stories (created on Boot Camp steps 20 and 21) while using the RACE method with an ally.

The following instructions are a repeat of step 20, except that you will use your second racial progress and unconscious bias stories. If you were not able to create those, then do the RACE method with a different ally than before.

A possible alteration that you might make is varying your relaxation methods and Listening Tips and paying attention to how they affect you.

Execution

1. Open the conversation by asking if racism against POC remains a problem needing attention. Before you do this, do a relaxation method and identify a Listening Tip you will use.

2. Whatever they say, ask them for experience that animates their view. Listen attentively and make them feel heard.

3. If they respond as an ally (racism against POC is a bigger problem), tell them your unconscious bias story. This will serve as a Connect story, since it aligns with what they are likely to think. If your assessment is wrong and they are a skeptic, tell them your racial progress story, which will function as a Connect story.

4. After you finish your Connect story, transition to your other story, which will function as an Expand story. For an ally, this will be your racial progress story. For a skeptic, this will be your unconscious bias story.

5. If it feels right, close the conversation by offering that both things could be true: Racism could be diminished, and it could still be a big problem.

Reflections

Which relaxation method did you use? How well did it work?

Which Listening Tip did you use? How well did it work?

Your perspective on racial progress?

Your perspective about people at different places on the continuum of racial bias?

Are there notable insights that you want to keep in mind as you progress to the next several steps?

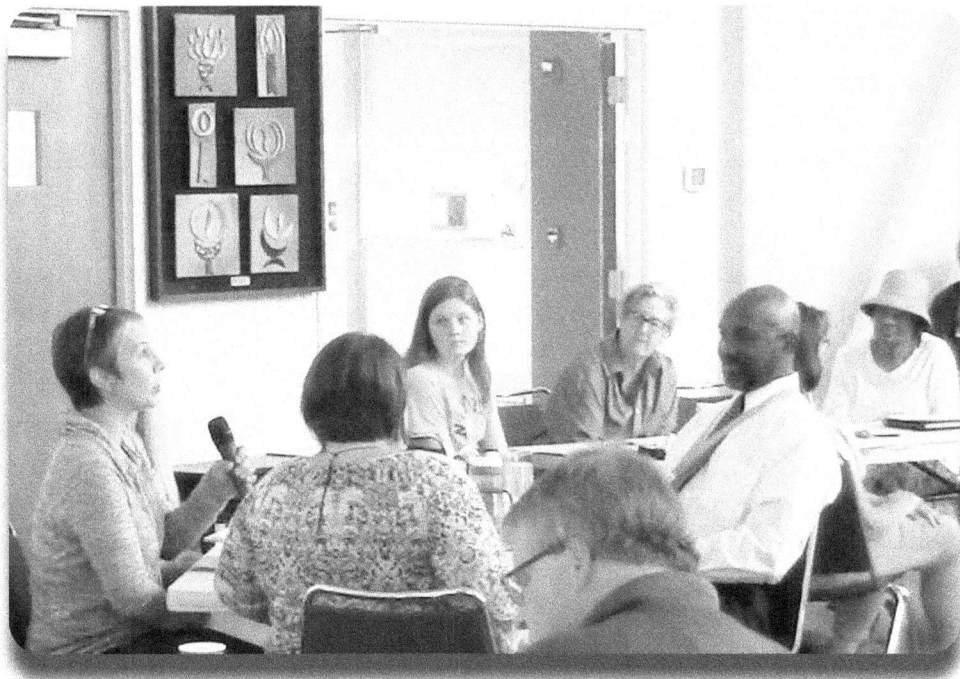

Closing

"No pain that we suffer, no trial that we experience is wasted. It ministers to our education, to the development of such qualities as patience, faith, fortitude and humility." — Orson F. Whitney

Date / /

Step 23

RACE Method With Secondary Stories To An Ally

"The more you leave out, the more you highlight what you leave in."
— Henry Green

Grounding — 7th Principle:
Respect for the interdependent web
of all existence of which we are a part.
Stone 2: "All relations between persons ought ideally
to rest on mutual, free consent and not on coercion." We freely
choose to enter into relationships with one another.

Step 23's Objective
- Deploy your second racial progress and unconscious bias stories with someone you predict will be an ally.

Because being a Compassionate Warrior is rooted 100% in compassionate listening, the goal at this point is for you to be spiritually grounded in all your interactions with compassion at the center. This step's task is to use your developed compassion-based dialogue skills with someone you agree with about race, while intentionally sharing your Connect stories — not to connect with them, but to get comfortable admitting that you have some things in common with racism skeptics. This will result in an interesting and hopefully vibrant interaction with your ally, one in which they may realize they, too are not completely different from skeptics. Be prepared to use your calming techniques, as the ally may have strong reactions to what you share. The goal is for you to manage the conversation without losing your cool, without dodging the opportunity to share your Connect story, and without being overcome with shame that you have something in common with racism skeptics. Remember, racial awareness is a journey on a path with a wide range of allies. We are all at different places on the path.

We aspire to a world where people are valued for their humanity. Not seeing others as a commodity, or a means to an end, and where the authenticity of freely chosen relationships as a core value is our ideal, but racism and unconscious bias are adversely affecting that goal and keeping us apart. You are becoming a warrior in the fight to change that.

This step, you will extend your soul to your ally as you share; first by listening to them deeply, and then by responding to them in a way that lets them know that you have an experience that resonates. If you are successful in forging a moment of authentic connection, the fact that you started talking to them as an exercise matters not. What does matter is the degree to which you feel a connection to this person by the time the conversation is over, and what you both have learned.

How would you assess how much the person felt heard? They:
☐ Felt Kinda Heard | ☐ Felt Heard | ☐ Felt Very Heard

How smooth was your questioning about their point of view and experience?
☐ Very Smooth | ☐ Smooth | ☐ Kinda Smooth/Kinda Clunky | ☐ Clunky | ☐ Very Clunky

How smooth was your transition to your Connect story, and how well did you tell it?
☐ Very Smooth | ☐ Smooth | ☐ Kinda Smooth/Kinda Clunky | ☐ Clunky | ☐ Very Clunky

How smooth was your transition to your Expand story, and how well did you tell it?
☐ Very Smooth | ☐ Smooth | ☐ Kinda Smooth/Kinda Clunky | ☐ Clunky | ☐ Very Clunky

How did you close the encounter?

What are your big takeaways from this experience?

If your assessment of them as an ally or skeptic was inaccurate, what are your reflections on the factors that created your incorrect assessment?

Closing

"Do your little bit of good where you are; it's those little bits of good put together that overwhelm the world."
— Desmond Tutu

Date / /

Step 24

Get Feedback
from Your Boot Camp Buddy and ANA Role Play

"In a growth mindset, challenges are exciting rather than threatening.
So rather than thinking, oh, I'm going to reveal my weaknesses, you say,
wow, here's a chance to grow." — Carol Dweck

Grounding — 4th Principle:
A free and responsible search for truth and meaning.
Stone 1: "Religious liberalism depends on the principle that
'revelation' is continuous." Our religious tradition is a living
tradition because we are always learning new truths.

Step 24's Objectives
- Practice your stories with your Boot Camp buddy and get feedback.
- Do a role play with your buddy playing the role of a skeptic in your circle.

Take a moment to think about how this process has changed or influenced the way you engage with everyone in your life. Do you feel empowered to have a positive impact on all your relationships by being more compassionate? Building your capacity for compassion is a singular endeavor. Growing as a communicator, however, is dependent on you engaging others and listening to feedback.

This step's task may feel like the most unnatural of any step of this Boot Camp. It will involve engaging a friend in giving you some feedback on your storytelling as well as engaging them in some role-playing.

Do not be put off if this process feels uncomfortable or strange. The wisdom of the universe is sometimes in plain sight. It is sometimes found in moments of great beauty or great ugliness; sometimes, as with this step, this transcendent wisdom comes from situations that feel just plain weird. As we strive toward becoming our best selves, a key task is to not put constructions around the sources of our wisdom and enlightenment. None of us knows enough to accurately predict the next moment of insight. That is why we call it "faith."

Our task is to be ever vigilant and always open to the light of clarity and wisdom, even from unusual sources.

Assignment

This step's set of tasks is the longest in the entire Boot Camp. You will need about 30 minutes of the time of a Boot Camp buddy. The exercises will involve you practicing your stories and role playing the Apologetic Non-Apology.

Part 1: Feedback on Your Stories

1. Explain to your Boot Camp buddy that you want to get feedback on your two secondary stories. Show them the feedback questions below.
2. Explain how the RACE method works if you haven't previously. Start with the longer version of your secondary stories.
3. After you get feedback, retell the stories and attempt to integrate their feedback.
4. If possible, discuss ways you might modify the telling if you are telling it at a much shorter duration.
5. Move to the secondary stories.

Here are the questions that your buddy should touch on in addition to other feedback that might come to their mind:

1. How compelling is the story?

2. How well do you draw the listener in as you tell it?
3. Are there any nuances or subtleties that are likely to generate resistance or engagement by racism skeptics?
4. How smooth or awkward is your transition between the stories? Is there any way to improve it?

Part 2: Apologetic Non-Apology Role-Play

On step 15, you prepared the ANA for one or two people with whom you have had a difficult racial conversation. This step, you will build on that preparation and do a role-play with your ally partner playing the role of the skeptic. This will work MUCH better in-person than if you do this on the telephone or through the computer. However, either of those is superior to just imagining talking to the skeptic and talking to the mirror, which you have already done.

Here is the conversation sequence:

You: Nice to see you again, friend.

Friend: *(played by your Boot Camp buddy)*: Nice to see you.

You: I have been thinking about a conversation we had a while back. Can we take a second to talk about it?

Friend: Sure.

You: Remember when we were talking about *(the topic)*?

Friend: Yes

You: I was thinking about it the other day, and I realized that:

- *(Part 1 – Accountability for the Past)* I was *(some description of something you did that was unhelpful to connectedness)*.
- *(Part 2 – Vulnerability in the Present)* Even now as I talk about it, I am feeling *(how you think you will feel)*.
- *(Part 3 – Commitment to Better Behavior and More Questions in the Future)* So I want to say that if we talk about this again, I am committed to not doing that. And if we speak of this again, I want to ask you about your experiences related to this. Is that okay?

After this, debrief the experience with your friend. Answer these questions:
- How did each you feel about the exercise?
- What adjustments need to be made with respect to what you can expect to feel when you actually talk to the skeptic?
- Are there any other lessons that you should take away?
- In addition, give your friend a moment to comment on the process.

Do the same exercise again, focusing on a different skeptic.

Reflections on Part 1: Feedback on Stories

Did anything your Boot Camp buddy said about your stories surprise you?

How successful were you in making adjustments based on feedback? Were there adjustments that you found yourself resisting?

Do you favor any of your four stories over the others? Why? Do you have thoughts about which to deploy in what situations?

What other guidelines/lessons should you keep in mind as you make decisions about using these stories as you attempt to influence people?

Reflections on Part 2: ANA Role-Play

What lessons do you take from this process?

How did you feel during the process compared to how you thought you would feel?

Having done this, do you want to change the topic or change the skeptic you will approach before the end of the Boot Camp?

Closing

Do you need anybody?
I need somebody to love
Could it be anybody?
I want somebody to love
Oh, I get by with a little help from my friends.
— John Lennon and Paul McCartney

Date / /

Step 25

RACE Method With An Ally, Choosing Between Stories

"Only he who is well prepared has any opportunity to improvise."
— Ingmar Bergman

Grounding — 7th Principle:
Respect for the interdependent web
of all existence of which we are a part.

Step 25's Objectives
- Have a conversation with a likely ally using the RACE method.
- Make a choice in the moment about which two of your four stories you will use.

The key to making this step a success is to practice making an in-the-moment decision about which stories to marshal as you attempt to forge a transformative connection with someone. Remember that we work on the capacity to learn to make spontaneous adjustments out of recognition that spreading compassion is not a routinized process. To be most effective in any action, particularly one based on empathy and connectedness, we must be very attuned to subtle realities, forces, and even vibrations that may change moment to moment. Making appropriate adaptations is key. Use your relaxation methods. Stay grounded.

Make these adaptations out of recognition of the way that one moment influences the next and the way that one being influences the other, including us. Ideally, we need to be like lighthouses — strong beacons of commitment to compassion, steadfast and never wavering from our commitment to dismantling racism. But we also must be like kaleidoscopes — as we refract the light of those who disagree with us about race and racism, we are always changing and ever transforming because of the exigencies of the moment. Our commitment to making changes according to the needs of the moment reflects our deeper sense that we are no greater or less than anyone else, but rather that we are all connected, and it will take all of us to change the current reality.

Assignment

This step you will use the RACE method with an ally. Unlike recent Boot Camp steps, you will make a choice in the moment on which stories you will tell from your arsenal. This will push you one more step toward being able to flexibly manage a conversation with a skeptic.

The goal of this initiative is not to make you a robot but rather a fluid manager of productive conversation. Improvisational thinking is important. At this point, you have practiced both sets of your stories more than once. This step's task is to have a conversation with an ally where you decide in the moment which anecdotes you will share.

Preparation

Make a mental plan about which ally in your circle you will engage this step. Review the main points of all your stories.

1. Remind yourself that you are choosing someone with whom you likely agree about racial issues.
2. If possible, do not tell the person that this conversation is part of a class you are taking. If you can, just approach it as a regular conversation.

Execution

3. Just before your encounter, do a relaxation method and choose a Listening Tip.
4. Open the conversation by asking their perspective about racism, as you have previously during the Boot Camp.
5. Listen empathetically, making sure they feel heard. Notice how well your Listening Tip works for you.
6. Choose whichever story feels right for your Connect story. (If this person is an ally, it will be one of your unconscious bias stories or your unearned racial advantage story.) After an appropriate segue, tell an Expand story. (If they are an ally, this should be a racial progress or bigot story).
7. Shortly after the encounter, take a moment to make some mental or written notes.
8. Feel free to congratulate yourself in some way that feels appropriate. You have made a big step forward!

Reflections

• Which relaxation method did you use? How well did it work?

• Which Listening Tip did you use? How well did it work?

• How would you rate your listening?

How smooth was your questioning about their point of view and experience? What made it that way?
☐ Very Smooth | ☐ Smooth | ☐ Kinda Smooth/Kinda Clunky | ☐ Clunky | ☐ Very Clunky

How smooth was your transition to your Connect story, and how well did you tell it?
☐ Very Smooth | ☐ Smooth | ☐ Kinda Smooth/Kinda Clunky | ☐ Clunky | ☐ Very Clunky

How smooth was your transition to your Expand story, and how well did you tell it?
☐ Very Smooth | ☐ Smooth | ☐ Kinda Smooth/Kinda Clunky | ☐ Clunky | ☐ Very Clunky

How did you close the encounter?

What are your big takeaways from this experience?

Upon reflection, would you choose the same stories in the future for both Connect and Expand? Why or why not?

What adjustments would you make to any point in the sequence?

Closing

"I have found the paradox, that if you love until it hurts, there can be no more hurt, only more love."
— Mother Teresa

Step 26

RACE Method With An Ally, Choosing Between Stories, After Adjustments

"The pursuit of perfection often impedes improvement." — *George Will*

Grounding — Stone 1:
"Religious liberalism depends on the principle that 'revelation' is continuous." Our religious tradition is a living tradition because we are always learning new truths.

Step 26's Objectives
- Review the adjustments that you said were important to consider from step 25.
- Engage someone you anticipate is an ally, and implement the RACE method, making an improvisational choice about which stories to use.

Discipline means a way to train the mind by engaging in practice. Spiritual discipline is required to calm our thoughts, find fortitude, and begin again in love. The term "continuous improvement" is usually used for organizational processes, but we can also apply it to our spiritual path. Our aim is to be always striving toward being even more effective agents of compassion in our circle, extending more compassion to those we love, to those whose behavior or thoughts we dislike, and even to ourselves.

As we pay attention to our actions, we are always subject to surprises in both how well and poorly our actions match our goals. Sometimes we will go to new levels of effectiveness in some ways while simultaneously regressing on some other important domains. We need not experience this as frustrating. Instead, we can reframe our very nonlinear path toward improvement, reminding us that life is mysterious and always filled with interesting surprises.

Our willingness to make adjustments and changes for the sake of improvement is an important tool to help make our other compassion tools even more effective.

This step is the last practice step with the RACE method before you purposely use it to engage a skeptic.

Assignment
The primary difference between this step and step 25 is that you have a chance to make adjustments based on your own reflections from the previous experience. Consider trying different relaxation methods and Listening Tips.

Go into the encounter with a plan to use the stories you did NOT use on step 25. However, if something happens in the encounter that pushes you to tell one or more of the stories you used on step 25, do what feels most suitable.

Preparation

- Make a mental plan about which ally in your circle you will engage this step. Review the main points of all your stories.
- Remind yourself that you are choosing someone with whom you likely agree about racial issues.
- If possible, do not tell the person that this conversation is part of a class you are taking. If you can, just approach it as a regular conversation.

Execution

1. Just before your encounter, do a relaxation method and choose a Listening Tip.
2. Open the conversation by asking their perspective about racism, as you have previously done.
3. Listen empathetically, making sure they feel heard. Notice how well your Listening Tip works.
4. Plan to use the stories you DID NOT use on step 25, but let the situation dictate your final choice.
5. Shortly after the encounter, take a moment to make some mental or written notes.

Reflections

Which relaxation method did you use? How well did it work?

Which Listening Tip did you use? How well did it work?

How would you rate your listening?

How smooth was your questioning about their point of view and experience? What made it this way?
☐ Very Smooth | ☐ Smooth | ☐ Kinda Smooth/Kinda Clunky | ☐ Clunky | ☐ Very Clunky

How smooth was your transition to your Connect story, and how well did you tell it?
☐ Very Smooth | ☐ Smooth | ☐ Kinda Smooth/Kinda Clunky | ☐ Clunky | ☐ Very Clunky

How smooth was your transition to your Expand story, and how well did you tell it?

☐ Very Smooth | ☐ Smooth | ☐ Kinda Smooth/Kinda Clunky | ☐ Clunky | ☐ Very Clunky

How did your close the encounter?

What are your big takeaways from this experience?

Upon reflection, would you choose the same stories in the future for both Connect and Expand? Why or why not?

What adjustments would you make to what you did at any point in the sequence?

Closing

"You have to make mistakes to find out who you aren't. You take the action, and the insight follows: You don't think your way into becoming yourself."
— Anne Lamott

Date / /

Step 27

RACE Method With Skeptic

"A man would do nothing, if he waited until he could do it so well that no one would find fault with what he has done." — *Cardinal Newman*

Grounding — 1st Principle:
The inherent worth and dignity of every person;
2nd Principle: Justice, equity and compassion in human relations.

Step 27's Objective
- Successfully deploy RACE method with someone who is a racism skeptic.

In many ways, this step is like a Graduation Day. Thus, it is a good time to revisit core motivations. Are you ready to risk some social capital by engaging in an honest conversation that might have tense moments? Even though your approach is rooted in compassion, you will be talking about a hot-button issue with someone you know you disagree with.

This Boot Camp is rooted in recognition that the best way to influence white people who might deny compassion or understanding or opportunity to people of color is to extend compassion to those white folks themselves. We are motivated at a fundamental level by our commitment to justice and equity and our knowledge that all human beings matter equally and that the world we live in should reflect that but does not. We are willing to try and change that.

Goal

ACT defines a successful encounter with a racism skeptic as one where you get to be yourself for some or all of the interaction, and they leave the conversation not being completely disinterested in talking to you or another ally about race or racism at some future point.

You are in a strong position to create an effective encounter. You have practiced how to center yourself, how to ask experience questions, and how to listen. You have also developed and practiced two Connect stories a skeptic is likely to resonate with and two Expand stories about your direct connection to the problem of societal racism. **You got this.**

Preparation

- Choose the skeptic you hope to engage, as well as a backup skeptic. It may make sense not to choose the most hardened racist you know. To lessen the risk of your being triggered and thrown off center, make a plan to engage someone whose views bother you, not someone whose views you find completely abhorrent.
- Before you approach them, do a relaxation method. Remind yourself of your Listening Tip.

Execution

1. Use whatever conversation openers you think will engage them while not putting them on the defensive. Consider that they may be expecting you to judge them.
2. As you go through the Ask, Connect, and Expand steps, pay attention to how well you are executing the method as well as the impact on them.
3. Pause to reflect and assess as soon as you can after the encounter. Take mental or written notes.
4. Other important things to remember: Approach the conversation with a strategy, but have flexibility. This applies to your stories, and the ways that you will attempt to create a sense of connection in other ways.

Reflection

Which relaxation method did you use? How well did it work?

Which Listening Tip did you use? How well did it work?

How would you rate your listening?

How smooth was your questioning about their point of view and experience?
☐ Very Smooth | ☐ Smooth | ☐ Kinda Smooth/Kinda Clunky | ☐ Clunky | ☐ Very Clunky

How smooth was your transition to your Connect story, and how well did you tell it?
☐ Very Smooth | ☐ Smooth | ☐ Kinda Smooth/Kinda Clunky | ☐ Clunky | ☐ Very Clunky

How smooth was your transition to your Expand story, and how well did you tell it?
☐ Very Smooth | ☐ Smooth | ☐ Kinda Smooth/Kinda Clunky | ☐ Clunky | ☐ Very Clunky

How did you close the encounter?

What are your big takeaways from this experience?

Upon reflection, would you choose the same stories in the future for both the Connect and Expand steps. Why or why not?

Closing

"I truly believe that everything that we do and everyone that we meet is put in our path for a purpose. There are no accidents; we're all teachers — if we're willing to pay attention to the lessons we learn, trust our positive instincts and not be afraid to take risks or wait for some miracle to come knocking at our door."
— Marla Gibbs

Date / /

Step 28

RACE Method With a Skeptic, After Adjustments

"If your want peace, you don't talk to your friends. You talk to your enemies." — Desmond Tutu

Grounding — Stone 5:
"Liberalism holds that the resources (divine and human) that are available for the achievement of meaningful change justify an attitude of ultimate optimism." Hope.

Step 28's Objectives
- Clarify opportunities for improvement from your performance on step 26.
- Execute the RACE method, making the adjustments you intended.

This step we begin again. Whether your prior step's attempt to use the RACE method went swimmingly or was laughably ineffective, there is no doubt room for you to make improvements. Becoming a warrior of and for compassion is lifelong work. Our commitment to doing that work is fundamentally grounded in a sense that not only can we be better, but also that the world can be made better. Our task this step is to integrate our reflections on our previous use of new conversational strategies, to make some adjustments, and try again. We do this out of a sense that perfection may always be elusive but better is always possible.

Assignment

Your goal this step is essentially the same as step 27—to engage a conversation with someone you assess beforehand is a racism skeptic. Before you do that, you will take some notes on possible improvements from step 27. The goal is to try to implement those improvements and note the success of your attempt.

By making an adjustment this step, you will further solidify in your spirit that what you are doing is a personal practice you are attending to and moving slowly toward mastery over. Both of these are useful to experience as this Boot Camp ends and you are not propelled with a daily instruction.

98 | Step 28

Preparation

Write down some changes that you plan to make when you deploy the RACE method:

Subtask	Adjustment I will make
Relaxing before the encounter	
Choosing a Listening Tip	
Asking a question about experience	
Connect—telling a story the person likely agrees with	
Expand telling a story that will invite the person to new thinking	

Reflection

Which relaxation method did you use? How well did it work?

Which Listening Tip did you use? How well did it work?

How would you rate your listening?

How smooth was your questioning about their point of view and experience?
☐ Very Smooth | ☐ Smooth | ☐ Kinda Smooth/Kinda Clunky | ☐ Clunky | ☐ Very Clunky

How smooth was your transition to your Connect story, and how well did you tell it?
☐ Very Smooth | ☐ Smooth | ☐ Kinda Smooth/Kinda Clunky | ☐ Clunky | ☐ Very Clunky

How smooth was your transition to your Expand story, and how well did you tell it?
☐ Very Smooth | ☐ Smooth | ☐ Kinda Smooth/Kinda Clunky | ☐ Clunky | ☐ Very Clunky

How did you close the encounter?

What are your big takeaways from this experience?

Upon reflection, would you choose the same stories in the future for both Connect and Expand? Why or why not?

If you planned to make any adjustments on any of the above, make a note of the degree to which you executed the adjustments and what happened.

Closing

> "Success may require a lot of steps.
> But progress only requires one." — T. Jay Taylor

Date / /

Step 29

Executing An Apologetic Non-Apology

"When you forgive, you free your soul. But when you say I'm sorry, you free two souls." — Donald L. Hicks

Grounding — Stone 4:
We deny the immaculate conception of virtue and affirm the necessity of social incarnation." Agency: Good things don't just happen, people make them happen.

Step 29's Objectives
* Rehearse the ANA in the mirror.
* Talk to a skeptic you have a healed relationship with and deploy the ANA.

This step we attempt to reboot a relationship that has been harmed by something we thought or did. It is a step of renewal and rebirth!

In taking the bold step of owning up to our role in a past rift, we affirm our sense of agency over the course of human relations. We are expressing our belief that disconnections between people are not primarily a function of the inevitable ebb and flow of life. Rather, this step is a demonstration of our belief that a sense of ongoing communion with others is something that can be chosen and pursued through purposeful actions.

By taking action this step, we posit a truth that lies in tension with the adage "Time Heals All Wounds." Instead, our action reaffirms a less well-known competing and perhaps superior truth: "Only acts of healing, actively pursued, heal wounds."

Goal

The goal of the ANA is to use a past tough conversation about race as a springboard to not only heal a relationship but also improve potential future conversations about race or about other issues.

One feature of deploying the ANA is that you can make strategic choices about how far you want the interaction to go.

Specifically, the core part of the ANA ends with you letting the person know that if you talk about the topic again, you want to 1) not repeat the bad thing you did before and 2) ask them about their experiences related to the topic.

After you deliver the ANA soliloquy, you have will likely have at least three options:

Option 1: Signal that you feel the exchange has been completed and exit the conversation. This is a perfectly reasonable choice, especially since you just told them you are feeling at least a bit vulnerable. Note that you have the option of reopening the previous conversation about the topic, but you don't have to.

Option 2: Reopen the conversation partially. If you want to, you can build on the permission they have granted to ask about their experience, and ask them about their experience. It is also possible that they will launch into discussing their point of view without being asked. If they talk about their opinion, redirect them to their experience that drives their opinion.

- If they just start giving their experience that drives their opinion, you are in a good position to attentively listen, since you have been practicing this through the Boot Camp.
- After they tell their experience, you can thank them and exit the conversation. If they seem like they want to be combative, or the topic is far afield from stories you have, or for any other reason, you can say you want to percolate on their story and exit the conversation.

Option 3: If it feels like you have Connect and Expand stories suitable to the moment, you can proceed with the RACE method.

Assignment

Since early in the Boot Camp you have been working toward doing an Apologetic Non-Apology. For the past two Boot Camp steps, the task has been to use the RACE method with someone with whom you may not have experienced a disconnection around race before.

Preparation

- Review your notes from step 16 and choose which skeptic you plan to engage this step. Do whatever it takes to arrange an encounter with the person.
- Rehearse your ANA in the mirror.
- Before and after you do this, do your favorite relaxation technique.
- Remember which Listening Tip you want to use. Because this is a person you have a relationship with, there might be other Listening Tips than the ones you experimented with that might work better. Review steps 2, 9, 16 to see all the tips in three categories.
- As you go into the encounter, make decisions about how far you think it will go, but do not get overly attached to this decision. Give yourself psychological room to push forward or to pull back if you think you need to during the encounter.
- Try to take notes about what happened as soon after the encounter as possible.

Execute

For this step you will do the ANA, and depending on your choices in the moment, you might further the reconciliation by completing the entire RACE method.

Reflections

How did you feel during the process compared to what you thought you would feel?

What appeared to be the impact of the ANA on the person?

How do you feel about your choice in the moment to go as far as you chose to take the conversation?

Overall, is there any notable change in how your relationship with this person feels?

Were there any other impacts of this experience worth noting?

Closing

"We must develop and maintain the capacity to forgive. He who is devoid of the power to forgive is devoid of the power to love. There is some good in the worst of us and some evil in the best of us. When we discover this, we are less prone to hate our enemies."
— Martin Luther King, Jr.

Step 30

Preparing To Sustain The Journey

"If you want to go fast, go by yourself. If you want to go far, go with others" — African Proverb

Grounding — 6th Principle:
The goal of world community
with peace, liberty, and justice for all.

Step 30's Objective

- Think about allies who might be useful supports to your RACE Method Practice.
- Think about people whom you might want to tell about your Boot Camp experience.
- Read the closing commentary about different ways of talking about this experience.

Anti-racism as spiritual practice is at the heart of being a Compassionate Warrior. This step we will focus on putting a few things in place that will help sustain our lifelong journey of using conversations about racial equity as key parts of our work on spreading compassion to the world. If we commit to continually engaging with this thorny issue for the rest of our lives, it is important to be able to sustain ourselves. Fundamentally, we engage in the work of racial equity because we reject the way that race has been positioned to create poisonous rifts in the human family. Our recognition of the oneness of humanity drives us to add our energies toward efforts aimed at allowing people from all groups to experience full liberty and justice. We chose this path both because all people –even ones we disagree with – deserve to have peace and compassion, but also because we know that compassion and peace are contagious. We choose the path of spreading compassion with these methods because we believe that every person and community that has been harmed by racism will be healed by the hope of compassion and the resiliency of love. Everyone should experience peace along with liberty and justice. We engage this work because we strive to live in peaceful community with those who would deny a full measure of peace, liberty, and justice to others based on their race or ethnicity. We can win the war on racism by being Compassionate Warriors.

Goal

Congratulations! You have completed an important journey of improved competence skills in deploying compassion-based strategies in the fight to dismantle racism. And you are also at the beginning of another journey to improve your competence. This step's task is primarily one of reflection and planning for step 31 and beyond.

Managing Your Own Journey

The nature of the ally's path is that it is optional. Anti-racism allies choose how much energy they want to spend on dismantling racism; they can choose anywhere from "never" to "occasionally" to "every waking moment". One factor that will most likely keep you actively engaging the ally path is to be in some regular communication with other people who look at being a better ally as an important part of their personal mission. It will be useful to identify others who would not mind talking about the quality and quantity of their efforts to be forces opposing racism.

As noted on step 1, there are many dimensions of allyship, even though this initiative only focuses on talking to racism skeptics. At the end of this step's instruction, there is a tool that helps you think about several people in your circle and make an initial assessment as to who you might want to invite into an ally support group that you might start.

Once you have thought about the people who would be most important as supporters to your ally journey, think about ways to structure that support. For example, you might decide on a weekly text, a bi-weekly phone call, or a monthly meeting. The most important thing now is to think about the people who seem most suitable to providing mutual support on your journey toward more effective allyship.

Tools, Products, and Services

The initiative associated with this Boot Camp—the Ally Conversation Toolkit—is specifically designed to help anti-racism allies start and continue their journey. There is a good deal of free content on our public Facebook pages, YouTube channel, and www.allyconversationtoolkit.com. In addition, there are additional resources on the subscriber page; these resources include access to other people on a similar ally journey, automated video and written resources, and access to coaching. You are invited to avail yourself of the free and subscription resources.

Of course, this initiative is not the only resource that can be helpful to allies on their journey. Appendix 1 provides a list—inherently only partial and imperfect—of other resources that you might consider making a part of your ongoing ally journey.

The Bigger Context of Your Anti-Racism Ally Practice

If you have benefited from this experience, the initiative wants you to push yourself to spread the word about it to others. Of course, not everyone is a promoter, and many allies are introverts who are disinclined to energetically promote anything. Still this guide will close with a few brief comments about how you might think about and talk about your journey toward becoming a Compassionate Warrior against racism. As you talk to other white people who may wonder why you are engaged in this practice, these rationales may help them see that becoming actively engaged in ally work is not limited to the goal of creating more racial equity.

Personal and Spiritual Growth

This Boot Camp may have strengthened your ability to stay centered in challenging moments. Obviously, increasing your ability to stay centered is a good thing and can potentially have benefits outside of talking about racial issues. Focusing on staying centered and engaging people in ways that are based on compassion is a suggestion from spiritual teachers from almost every tradition. This edition of the book is purposely written to highlight the spiritual dimensions of anti-racism work, although this is not usually how anti-oppression work is usually talked about. Yet, this is a valid way of seeing what this work is about. Moreover, throwing more compassion in the world often has a multiplier effect, because when people receive compassion, they are more likely to extend compassion to others. In order to grow the anti-racism movement, there will be times when you can be an ambassador for a new way of thinking about what this work is. If you see your anti-racism ally journey as part of a larger process of personal and collective spiritual growth, don't be shy about talking about it in these terms.

Relationships

After immersing themselves in practices of compassion-based communication on one topic, many allies notice that it enhances their communications capacities on other issues. This improved skill, in turn, can have a healing effect on relationships, whether conflicts about race were a big or small part of those relationships. By improving your ability to engage compassionately and from a place of empathetic listening, you are likely to be a calming force countering the tensions at social gatherings that include people with whom you vehemently disagree. Given the way that current public and political issues often undermine family and other relationships and things as prosaic as Thanksgiving, you may become a force for comity at such settings. If you see your anti-racism ally journey as making it easier for families and friends to get along, don't be shy about talking about it in these terms.

American Political Culture

The Ally Conversation Toolkit is specifically devoted to dismantling various "isms" (racism, sexism, homophobia, etc.) that undermine America (and every other nation, for that matter). Our inability to talk about our nation's oldest problem is related to our increasing inability to cross ideological divides.

Let's remember, this inability is a national weakness that America's enemies are purposely trying to exploit for their own advantage. Any time an American learns how to purposely deploy compassion-based communication to productively engage with racism skeptics, a weakness in American political culture becomes a little less weak. If you see your ally journey as making the nation stronger, don't be shy about talking about it in these terms.

Increasing Your Discernment About Allies Who Can Help Your Journey

It is useful to think about which people in your circle – defined broadly – you might want to meet with regularly (say, bi-weekly or monthly) to talk about your influence practice.

First, think of the six folks that you would consider for your three-person racial ally support group. Write their names here:

1.	4.
2.	5.
3.	6.

In addition to typical factors you use to choose people, the following characteristics seem of particular importance.

- Willingness to try to push oneself past limitations
- Capacity to be reflective
- Graciousness to others (and oneself) when goals are not met
- Level of commitment to racial equity

Next you are going to analyze your list of potential ally practice supporters. Below is a table with the four characteristics above and a blank space for criteria that you might think is particularly important, too. As you rate the ally, compare them to other people who are allies in the broad definition of that word. (That is, it is OK if they have never gone to a White Ally meeting.)

Scale: 4 (strong) — 1 (weak)	Is willing to push themselves	Capacity to reflect	Graciousness	Commitment to racial equity
Person				
1.				
2.				
3.				
4.				
5.				
6.				

Reflections

In light of this exercise, which people seem most suitable to recruit to actively support your journey as an anti-racism ally?

Final Closing

"Infuse your life with action. Don't wait for it to happen. Make it happen. Make your own future. Make your own hope. Make your own love. And whatever your beliefs, honor your creator, not by passively waiting for grace to come down from upon high, but by doing what you can to make grace happen...yourself, right now, right down here on Earth." — Bradley Whitford

Thanks for your allyship and keep up the good work!

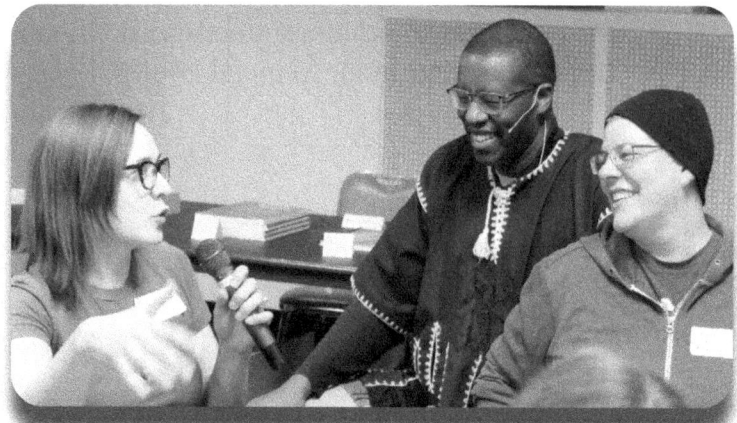

Appendix A: Resources
Other resources to enhance your journey towards using the RACE Method

There is a growing understanding of the important role that white people can play in dismantling racism. Accordingly, there are a growing number of resources that people can avail themselves of if they want some assistance for their journey toward greater insight and effectiveness in promoting racial equality.

This should be considered a very partial and extremely imperfect listing of the resources that are available. While most of these tools are specifically targeted toward white allies, some of them are intended to be of use to anyone in the anti-racism movement.

Web

- **Ally Conversation Toolkit** (www.allyconversationtoolkit.com)
  This is the initiative behind this *RACE Method Boot Camp*. The website and initiative have a number of resources available, including; *The White Ally Toolkit Workbook, The Discussion Leader Guide to the Workbook, The RACE Method Introductory Video Course, The Holiday Survive and Thrive Webinar.*
- **Racial Equity Tools** (www.racialequitytools.org)
  This very large and well-curated resource houses a variety of research tips, tools, and curricula to help those working toward justice in systems, organizations, communities, and culture at-large.

Books

- *White Ally Toolkit Workbook,* **by David Campt** (www.allyconversationtoolkit.com)
- *Living in the Tension,* **by Shelly Tochluk** (www.shellytochluk.com)
- *Witnessing Whiteness,* **by Shelly Tochluk** (www.shellytochluk.com)
- *White Fragility,* **by Robin DiAngelo** (www.robindiangelo.com)
- *What Does it Mean to be White: Developing White Racial Literacy,* **by Robin DiAngelo**
- *Waking up White,* **by Debby Irving** (www.debbyirving.com)
- *White Like Me,* **by Tim Wise** (@timjacobwise)

Guides for Regular Practice and Reflection

- *Understanding What It Means to be White and Privileged Journal,* **by Tom Schweizer**
- *21 Day Racial Equity Habit Building Challenge* (www.debbyirving.com/21-Day-challenge/)
- *Pointmade Daily Racial Equity Instagram* (www.instagram.com/pointmadelearning/)

Appendix B: RACE Method Discussion Guide (CWDG)

At-A-Glance Overview

Each congregation of followers has its own unique needs and dilemmas surrounding how to introduce and sustain new efforts. This at-a-glance resource helps with some of the decision-making around planning how to implement a new curriculum, providing some key considerations for forming learning groups to engage with the Boot Camp. Even though the steps of the Boot Camp are presented in the context of individual tasks that support greater anti-racism allyship, the Ally Conversation Toolkit (ACT) is based on the premise that most people will master these methods much faster if they are a part of a learning group that meets on a regular basis.

This guide presumes that you are a relatively experienced group leader, though not necessarily a religious leader. This guide also provides a model agenda for a meeting as a learning group, as well as an outline for some skill building exercises that might be used at various points in the Boot Camp. A large portion of this guide is aimed at helping you think through the numerous trade-offs between different ways of setting the learning group up and running it.

Recommendations for RACE Method Learning Groups

Size of Groups:	3 to 12 people
Duration of Meetings (not including fellowship time):	Between 50 minutes and 2 hours
Frequency of Meetings:	Between 2/week and 1/ month
Number of Meetings	Between 4 and 30*
Boot Camp Steps Between Meetings:	Between 2 and 8*
Duration of Learning Group Process	30 days to 15 months*
Age of Participants:	16 years and older
Audio-Visual Technology Needed?	No, though video can enhance
Are Remote Meetings Possible?	Yes*

*As will be discussed, these scheduling choices are highly dependent on each other.

The above ranges are rather wide, so Group Leaders will need to decide where to land within all these aspects of groups. Several of the considerations and trade-offs will be discussed extensively below.

Presumptions About the Group Leader

This guide is written with the expectation that the person who is leading a RACE Method discussion group will not necessarily be a clergy or religious leader, but will have had some prior experience in leading discussion groups, even if those groups were not focused on racism. This expectation of prior leadership experience is in contrast to another leaders' guide created by the ACT initiative. Specifically, the Discussion Group Leaders Guide (DGLG) is a supplement to the White Ally Toolkit Workbook, which itself is a much longer and more in-depth resource for developing allyship. The DGLG and RACE Method

Discussion Guide (CWDG) are very similar in terms of approaches on how to lead groups, but the CWDG is focused on the personal journey, while the DGLG is focused on helping group leaders effectively navigate the RACE methodology on a wide variety of topics. The DGLG is not written with the expectation that the group leader has any experience in leading groups through learning journeys. As a result, the DGLG gives much more detailed guidance about group management, including guidance about the ways to open meetings, instructions about making transitions, and other helpful information. If you are a novice group leader, and are looking for additional support in how to make a group study more effective, we recommend you invest in the DGLG; however, if you are an experienced group leader, this appendix will most likely suffice and this guide can help you run Boot Camp groups as Chalice Circles, Circle Meetings, or small group ministry groups.

This guide will not provide a great deal of advice about how to make the Learning Group feel like a Unitarian Universalist experience specifically, (or a spiritual meeting generally) beyond the guidance that is already articulated in the daily instructions. The assumption is that you have or can access guidance for how to do that. Most UU congregations have religious education leaders who know how to add the elements to a group meeting that are aligned with the way that such meetings are conducted within groups like this. It is worth noting, however, that if you are successful at creating collective spiritual atmosphere around these meetings that resonates with the participants, the group experience is likely to deepen people's connection to the content and lead to a transformational commitment to anti-racism work.

The next few pages review some factors to think about as you define the parameters of the group. As you review this feedback, be mindful that as of the writing of this document in Spring 2019, the ACT Initiative has gotten feedback about the group process from fewer than a dozen Learning Groups from around the country. The advice in this edition of the Guide is based on this feedback and more than four decades of experience from facilitators, but not on hundreds of groups, which hopefully will be the case in the near future. In fact, the ACT Initiative would love to hear feedback from you at info@whiteallytoolkit.com about the methods you use to keep your group engaged.

Positioning a Learning Group for Success

The core objective of setting up learning groups is to provide the right amount and quality of interaction with others so that each person engages with the material in a way that maximizes their learning. There are a number of logistical factors concerning the sequencing of the learning group meetings that have to be decided, but at this stage in the evolution of this initiative, there are no clear best practices. The purpose of the subsections below is to direct your attention to these factors, and to make sure that you are making conscious and informed choices about the trade-offs between different approaches.

Overall Duration of the Learning Group Course

The Boot Camp presents 30 steps under the premise that the tasks on most steps can be completed in 20-25 minutes, not including the reading about the task, which usually takes about five minutes. While there have been people who completed the entire sequence in as little as 30 days, this has been rare. Only a small portion of people can add a new 30-minute task to their schedule and consistently execute it, no matter how excited they are when they initially sign up to do so.

You will need to decide over what period of time you want to complete the course. If a group were to engage the content at a pace of a Boot Camp step each day, it would complete the entire Boot Camp in one month. For most people, it is more realistic to try to give oneself more than one day to complete each Boot Camp step assignment. The table below conveys how long it will take to complete 30 steps of assignments at several different paces.

2 days per Boot Camp step	60 days/about 2 months
3 days per Boot Camp step	90 days/about 3 months
4 days per Boot Camp step	120 days/about 4 months
5 days per Boot Camp step	150 days/about 5 months
6 days per Boot Camp step	180 days/about 6 months
7 days per Boot Camp step	30 weeks/about 7 months

If your group schedule is at the more frequent end of this spectrum, the people in the group may be at risk for slipping into non-completion because the demands are simply too great on people's daily schedule. Very few people can add a new demand to their daily schedule and consistently spend 20-25 minutes on it. On the other hand, if your pace through the Boot Camp is too slow, people may disengage from the material because they may not have the internal and group pressure to stick with the process so that they can report results at the next meeting.

It may be most useful to survey the group about its desires on this question and to occasionally have an honest conversation about how much they are engaging the material compared to what they expected of themselves. Your group may need to make adjustments one way or another if the pace is not well-suited to collective engagement and success. For Unitarian Universalists and other covenantal religious groups, it may be helpful to make a promise to one another about your intentions to engage with the materials and to be present at the meetings. Accountability is an important part of anti-racism work and practicing calling each other back into the work as white allies is important. Remember that people of color never get a day off from living with the effects of racism.

The Pace of Progress Through the Boot Camp Steps

The pace of progress through the 30 Boot Camp steps just discussed is related to but different than the issue of how frequently the group meets. To illustrate, a group that is progressing through the document at two Boot Camp steps per week might meet weekly, every other week, monthly, or every other month. The conversations in these meetings would be very different, and the range of tasks they would be expected to reflect on would be very different.

Clearly, you want to avoid a situation where a sizable number of people stop showing up because the meetings are too frequent. On the other hand, if there is too long a lapse between meetings, people will have less of a sense they are on a group journey where they are supporting each other's incremental progress through the material.

One group threaded this needle in an interesting way. The group chose a pace of two Boot Camp steps per week and would meet monthly. The expectation was that at each meeting, people would discuss their progress over eight Boot Camp steps; the course would be completed in about four months. However, each participant was expected to meet every other week with a Boot Camp buddy from the group. Thus, the expectation was that each person was committing to attending eight meetings over four months, with four of those meetings being specifically scheduled with one other person.

Length of Meetings

No matter how frequent the meetings are, it is important that each meeting achieve a good balance between 1) "content time" —focused moments of reflection, accountability with self-examination, and skill building, and 2) "fellowship time" that helps to establish and solidify camaraderie. Later in this appendix, you will see a sample meeting agenda for the content time of the meeting.

This model agenda is based on the assumption that you are allocating about 80 minutes for the "content time." It is not recommended that the content time be constructed to be shorter than 50 minutes, since it has a number of elements that are important.

Group leaders should think about creating a good balance between fellowship time and content time. The experiences of several groups suggest that some time purely devoted to fellowship is important to overall group success. A number of participants have told group leaders that they very much appreciate being in a setting where they don't have to worry about people making deeply racially problematic statements and where they can talk about the myriad struggles of being an anti-racism ally. Being able to relax and not worry about how people will handle racial topics is comforting to a significant portion of allies.

On the other hand, it must be said that some groups have reported that fellowship can sometimes be so compelling that it can overtake the entire convening if the group leader is not careful. It may be useful to explicitly make the group aware of the need to balance both types of time, so that people work with you to make sure the group is balancing these elements.

As one might predict, having a meal as part of the fellowship time enhances the fellowship, but increases the risk of the content time being crowded out of the agenda before people have to leave the meeting.

Size of Group

Generally, the project recommends that the core group size be no more than ten to twelve people, though a few groups have had more than this number. It is important that the group size be large enough so that it is likely that at least one person has something very positive to report each meeting. Strong success stories have a catalytic effect on everyone. But the group should be small enough so that there is ample opportunity for each person to express their experience of trying to engage the RACE Method out in the world between the meetings.

One group used an innovative meeting structure that is useful if your group has a medium size meeting space and more than twelve people who want to be involved. The group had a monthly meeting of all of the interested participants. The meeting had a short time at the start and the end where all the participants were gathered together. After the meeting was initiated, separate groups of ten or fewer met in breakout sessions. There was some time when the groups reconvened in plenary before the overall meeting was adjourned. This structure allowed retelling of some particularly successful stories that had emerged from the small group.

If a group has seven to twelve people it may be advantageous for group leaders to vary between times when people are in small groups and when the whole group is having one conversation. Whether and how often you manage a group of seven to twelve this way should be influenced by a few different factors, including the general facilitation skill in the group and time frame of the meeting. Remember: take time to evaluate your plan. The most important factor in determining the success of the content time of the learning groups is an honest and inclusive conversation about things that went well and went poorly. If there are ten people in the group and the group only has 45 minutes, the group leader may need to have the group discuss some issues in groups of three or four in order to ensure that everyone gets some time to talk about their triumphs and trials in attempting to engage the processes suggested in the Boot Camp.

In addition, when you break down a group into small subgroups that you are not directly managing, the risk is increased that everyone will not get a fair chance to express himself or herself. This is especially true if the group includes one or two people who are loquacious or who tend to stray from assigned tasks. Consider these factors as you make choices about when to stay in full group and when to not do that.

Age of Participants

The Boot Camp was not designed specifically to be used with adolescents or younger people. It is our opinion that youth enrolled in high school have most likely had enough encounters with race and racially problematic situations to benefit from this training. Some groups with relatively younger people are beginning to use it, though. As you know, many of the questions probe people for memories, and young people usually inherently have fewer of them. It may be a struggle for people under 30– and even more so for people under 20 – to find memories that include demonstrations of substantial racial progress or people freely expressing dramatically bigoted views, though they may have seen them in various forms of media. On the other hand, younger people often bring both a candor to the racial conversations and a higher level of racial literacy that can make conversations richer. Ideally, if teens are going to engage in the materials, it would be helpful for them be part of a multi-age group.

Meeting Online

If most members of the group have computer and internet access, it is possible to conduct the meetings over an internet link, using a platform like Zoom, Go To Meeting, or even telephone teleconference. Obviously, it will be even more important that you think about how to experience the benefits of interpersonal fellowship in meetings of this nature.

Integration of Other ACT Initiatives

A number of groups have productively integrated other materials from the Ally Conversation Toolkit Initiative into their group meetings.

For instance, the RACE Method Introductory video course is an 50-minute video course that can be watched all at once or sequentially in six short lessons; the separate lessons include one focused on the project background, one lesson for each step of the RACE method, and one lesson on the Apologetic Non-Apology. Each of the video lessons has worksheets and homework. Some groups have integrated the course into their progress through the RACE Method Boot Camp and the White Ally Toolkit Workbook. If your meetings take place in a venue with an easily visible computer monitor and an internet connection, integrating video into the learning group can significantly augment participants' experience.

The White Ally Toolkit Workbook provides a number of reflection tools that some group leaders have incorporated into their group meetings for the Boot Camp. For instance, one Boot Camp group leader was struggling to help a group member work through a hesitation that was impeding their progress. This ally was rather introverted and most of her social circle was very liberal. This combination of factors led the ally to conclude that it was "impossible" to find skeptics she could engage while using the methods. Since this leader was already familiar with the Workbook, she used an instrument in the Workbook focused on helping the ally see her own strong bias against conservatives. The insights generated by the instrument and the discussion were helpful in letting the ally find a rationale for pushing herself past the sense that she could not engage the project methods.

As noted, the Discussion Group Leaders Guide includes detailed instructions for the meetings that may be useful, especially for relatively novice group leaders. The appendix to that publication also has several brief biographies of white allies from different fields who have demonstrated significant actions for the cause of racial equity. The guide also provides suggestions for specific places within the meeting agenda where these biographies might be read and reflected on to inspire the group. These descriptions of white folks who have demonstrated great commitment to anti-racism allyship — some at the cost of their own lives — might be a useful inspiration at the right time in your learning group.

Use of Other Supplementary Materials

A number of groups have integrated this Boot Camp into an ongoing anti-racism book group that is also reading other important texts about race. As you consider how focusing on the Boot Camp might be positioned in relationship to other texts, try to differentiate the focus of different equity-focused books or trainings efforts based on whether they focus on:

- **Awareness** – helping allies see their personal role in the problem of race/racism
- **Knowledge** – helping allies understand the dynamics of race/racism in society
- **Skills** – helping allies become more proficient at taking relevant actions against racism

The Boot Camp and other offerings of the ACT Initiative focus precisely on skill-building– specifically the skill of 1-on-1 persuasion. The presumption of this project is that while it is useful for people to advance their awareness or knowledge about racism, **allies can immediately increase their persuasiveness with racism skeptics without waiting until they make advances in these other dimensions.**

Put differently, while you may want to place engagement with the Boot Camp within a sequence of engagements of other books, this project does not suggest that additional knowledge or awareness be presented as precursors to greater engagement of racism skeptics. In fact, there may be some risks in doing so, because some allies will interpret this sequence as encouragement to share their newfound understandings with racism skeptics, and this may be actually counterproductive.

At the same time, learning more and increasing self-awareness are valuable and can enhance one's overall effectiveness as an ally. The key is to be careful not to have allies misinterpret the relationship between: increased awareness processes, increased general knowledge on the subject, and the need for using one's privilege to influence racism skeptics. We focus on the latter because this situation is urgent.

The Learning Cycles of the Boot Camp

As you consider how frequently to hold learning group meetings, the pace of progress, and related matters, it is important to think through how the skill-building elements of each meeting fit into the participants' learning journey. Specifically, it is important to think through the role of skill-building activities during the meetings; if you are going to have these activities (all groups do not do this though we recommend it) you want to think through which skills you have participants work on at which meetings.

The argument for doing skill-building work during meetings is that the learning group setting is a great time for allies to practice skills that the Boot Camp will ask them to work on during the upcoming Boot Camp steps. This allows participants to get some initial experience: thinking about, planning, and even using these processes in the relative safety of a supportive group.

> Allyship is a long-life long commitment to making the world a better place. Being willing to learn more and more and engage effectively as a non-violent agent for change is personally transformational.

Accordingly, it is useful to see the pattern that the Boot Camp is based on. A table that summarizes the Boot Camp follows.

Step 1: Understanding the RACE Method

Step 2: Learning quick relaxation methods and Listening Tips	**Step 9:** Experimenting with new Listening Tip	**Step 16:** Listening attentively	**Step 23:** Race method with secondary stories with ally
Step 3 – Asking questions that focus on experiences beneath beliefs	**Step 10:** Listening to someone with whom you disagree	**Step 17:** Asking for the experience of a skeptic	**Step 24:** Get feedback from your Boot Camp buddy and ANA role play
Step 4: The Apologetic Non-Apology	**Step 11:** Planning the ANA	**Step 18:** Preparing for ANA for two skeptics	**Step 25:** RACE method with ally, choosing between stories
Step 5: Focus on the connection with skeptics in your circle	**Step 12:** Reflecting on racial progress	**Step 19:** Finding ideas you agree with	**Step 26:** RACE method with ally, choosing between stories, making adjustments
Step 6: Finding ideas you like embedded in perspectives you don't like	**Step 13:** Turning notes into usable anecdotes	**Step 20:** Develop a second Connect story	**Step 27:** RACE method with a skeptic
Step 7: Your experience of Unconscious bias	**Step 14:** Relaxing and telling your stories	**Step 21:** Develop a second Expand story	**Step 28:** RACE method with a skeptic, after adjustments
Step 8: Reflection and synthesis	**Step 15:** Reflection and synthesis	**Step 22:** Reflection and synthesis	**Step 29:** Executing an ANA
Step 30: Preparing to sustain the journey			

As you can see, excluding the first step, there is a pattern that is largely (but not perfectly) repeated over the first three weeks of the Boot Camp. After an introductory step, the first three weeks of the Boot Camp largely repeats the following sequence:

Relaxing and Listening	Steps 2, 9, 16
Asking Questions	Steps 3, 10, 17
Apologetic Non-Apology	Steps 4, 11, 18
Relating to Racism Skeptics	Steps 5, 12, 19
Opening Our Minds to Perspectives We Don't Like	Steps 6, 13, 20
Refining Our Story	Steps 7, 14, 21
Reflection and Synthesis	Steps 8, 15, 22

The last several steps do not follow the same pattern, since the activities are focused on bringing all the skills together.

You might consider how this pattern might affect your scheduling of meetings and what you focus on. For instance, one approach might be to arrange group meetings on Reflection and Synthesis steps, since this is largely what the meetings are intended to accomplish. On the other hand, there might be advantages in scheduling the meetings so that the Reflection and Synthesis steps are between meetings, which might serve to build in more reflection to the participants' journey through the Boot Camp.

As you are designing the way the participants will engage the Boot Camp, here are some additional points to keep in mind.

On step 2, the Boot Camp instructs participants to take notes on at least two skeptics they know. At the first or second group meeting, you can explain to participants that one benefit of the learning group is that they will have multiple opportunities to play the role of a skeptic so that their fellow allies can practice their methods. If they want to, they have the opportunity to repeatedly play the role of one of the skeptics they took notes about. They may find that doing so has the effect of increasing their empathy toward this person, even though they will be playing the role of this person making racially problematic statements and justifying them.

- Any time after step 3, it is reasonable to have participants work on their listening skills by having a partner play the role of a skeptic. In a group meeting that is before step 7, your skill building process should focus on relaxing, asking questions, and listening empathetically to a fellow ally playing the role of a skeptic.
- Since the allies form their first story on step 7 and do not form a second one until step 12, any meeting between these steps might do skill-building based on listening and telling one story.
- After step 12, it is reasonable to have the group members practice the full RACE method, since they will have already developed their Connect and Expand stories.
- If you are going to do some skill building on the Apologetic Non-Apology, it may make sense to do this between step 11 (when the participants have prepared it in writing) and step 24, when they will practice the ANA with a Boot Camp buddy but will not have the benefit of a group learning atmosphere.

A Sample Meeting Agenda

The following meeting agenda is presented not with the intention of having Learning Group Leaders follow it, but rather as a means for you to understand the rationale for each process, the learning objectives, and some possible processes that might be used to achieve those objectives.

The elements in this meeting are timed so that the content portion of the meeting could be completed in 80 minutes. The parentheses show potential durations of these processes if you needed to complete the content portion in 50 minutes.

1. **Get spiritually centered – 10 min (5)**
   Objectives:
   - Get the participants centered and calm
   - Remind participants of the spiritual foundation behind this work

   Possible Process
   - One minute of silence
   - Read aloud the quotation and Grounding for the step
   - Solicit participant comments about the spiritual significance of the step's task.

2. **Check-in – 15 min (10)**
   Objectives:
   - Provide a setting of group accountability for the way each person engaged/avoided opportunities to use Boot Camp methods
   - Tangibly experience the reality that people will not make perfect progress in their allyship

Possible Process:
- Give people two minutes to think of a triumph (success) and a trial (failure) in allyship since last meeting
- Solicit at least one story from each person. In a longer meeting, one option is to invite each person to tell a triumph and a trial. In a shorter meeting, one option is to hear a few stories of each type – perhaps alternating around the group - but with each person being expected to tell at least one Triumph or Trial.

3. **Relaxation and listening methods 10 min – (5)**
   Objectives:
   - Remind people that working on being centered and attentively listening to other people is a precursor to the success of any other techniques of this project.
   - Encourage people to advance their understanding of how they respond to various strategies designed to enhance relaxation and empathetic listening.
   Possible Process:
   - Group discussion
     - What listening tips have you tried since we last met?
     - What did you notice about what worked for you better and less well when listening to people?
     - What happened when you tried to listen to media sources that you dislike? What lessons did you learn about yourself from attempting to do so?

4. **Skills we worked on last meeting – how did it go? 15 min (10)**
   Objectives:
   - To provide a moment of accountability where people discuss how their real-world use of techniques focused on in the preceding meeting
   - To let each participant see the wide variety of ally success and failures in applying the material
   Possible Process:
   - Full group or sub-group discussion:
     - Were there any situations when you could have used the methods we worked on? To what extent did you attempt the methods?
     - How would you rate your degree of success on using the methods?

5. **Skill-building: practicing and getting ready for the upcoming tasks – 20 min (15)**
   Objectives
   - Give participants a chance to practice an important compassionate engagement skill in a safe environment
   - Have participants exercise their empathy muscles by having them play the role of a skeptic
   Possible Process:
   - In Appendices C, D, and E, there are three activities that outline a role-play exercise that may be useful at different points in the Boot Camp.
   - Worksheet 1: Practicing Listening may be particularly useful between step 3 and 7, after the participants have thought about their listening techniques before they have developed a Connect story.
   - Worksheet 2: RACE method through the Connect step may be particularly useful between step 7 and step 12, when the participants have worked on their Connect story but have not

developed an Expand story.
- Worksheet 3: RACE method through the Expand step may be particularly useful after step 12, when the participants have worked on both Connect and Expand stories.

6. **Closing inspiration – 5 min**
   Objectives
   - Provide an experience that ties the meeting together before the meeting adjourns
   - Reinforce the sense of connection between the participants
   - Foster a small bit of excitement about the journey they are continuing
   Possible Processes
   - Read the closing quotation for the step
   - Read short biography of a person

The following are websites that provide short biographies of Unitarians Universalists who have demonstrated a substantial commitment to freedom movements, including the racial equity movement
- www.uua.org/re/tapestry/adults/resistance/workshop11/182640.shtml
- www.mit.edu/people/fuller/unitarian.htm
- www.uudb.org/peace.html

How to Handle the Final Boot Camp Meeting

The last group meeting for a RACE Method Boot Camp has a number of goals that you should keep in mind:
- Celebrating people's progress in using the methods of the Boot Camp
- Acknowledging the accomplishment of completing the curriculum
- Encouraging continued engagement in learning about compassion-based methods
- Reinforcing the notion of lifelong anti-racism allyship and how the journey to becoming a better ally deepens one's understanding and practice of UUism

Celebrate Progress and Accomplishments

As you plan for the last meeting, it may be helpful to ritualize a way for the participants to collectively re-experience their progress since the start of the Boot Camp. One possible strategy is to give each person a small stone or marble, have them share some important positive change in themselves and them drop the stone in a vase filled with hand sanitizer (which has the perfect viscosity to allow the heavy object to silently and gently sink). Or perhaps you give two stones, one to use for a personal improvement and one for comments about changes/improvements that have seen in each other.

At some point, it will be useful for you as the group leader to congratulate the group for completing the process. Some groups have begun processes like this and not completed them, and your group may have lost members. Taking a moment to celebrate and recognize the fact that some members persevered will likely have a positive effect on the group.

It will be useful to remind them that not only have they completed something difficult, but because they completed the course, the world will become a little closer to what they want it to be — a more compassionate place.

Before the Meeting, Get Clear About Your Future Role

Before the meeting, it will be important to have done some prior thinking about your own willingness to continue serving as a group leader. Frequently, there is a substantial portion of the group who want to continue getting group support for continuing their journey toward greater ally effectiveness, though perhaps at a less frequent pace of meetings. It is helpful to for you as the leader to be clear about whether you want to play a role in this, which may look like leading a discussion group or finding another person willing to play a leadership role. If you have been successful as a group leader, it may be more important to start another Boot Camp Group, and perhaps the graduates for your group would all be willing to be leaders now. The goal is to bring as many people on-board with this project as possible.

Encourage Allies to Help Grow the Movement and Themselves

Don't forget to spend a moment on the possibility of the participant's recruiting other people into groups like this. The RACE Method movement needs people who are getting better and better at the methods, as well as new recruits. Think through a way to encourage the participants to invite others to this process and create a way to capture their interest in helping to increase momentum in the movement.

It is going to take all of us.

Welcome to RACE Method Anti-Racism Allyship!

Appendix C: Practicing Listening

A pair will do the exercise twice so each person has the chance to play both the ally and the skeptic.

Preparation

- Person in role of ally chooses which Listening Tip *(step 2)* they want to use.
- Person in role of skeptic chooses a skeptic they know *(step 1)* whose persona they will adopt. Get an idea of:
  - A belief they might have that reflects their being a skeptic.
  - A news source that the skeptic might quote.
  - An experience that the skeptic might bring up if asked for an experience related to their belief.

Implementation

Ally: "Hi, what has been on your mind recently?"

Skeptic: Make racially problematic belief statement

Ally: Mentally complete Listening Tip. Ask skeptic to say more about what they believe.

Skeptic: Elaborate on statement while referencing news source.

Ally: Mentally complete Listening Tip. Ask skeptic for an experience related to their belief.

Skeptic: Relate experience in a way that their skeptic might.

Ally: Listen empathetically. Paraphrase the story or use other strategy to convey to skeptic they have been heard clearly.

Reflections

Ally: How well did the Listening Tip work? How are you assessing that? How did listening to the belief and the story feel?

Skeptic: How much did the Ally make you feel heard? How did the exercise make you feel overall? Any lessons for you?

Switch Roles and Repeat

Appendix D: Practicing The RACE Method Through The *Connect* Step

Choose which person is going play the role of the skeptic first.

Prepare For Role Play (2 min)

Ally Preparation Tasks	Skeptic Preparation Tasks
Review worksheet, mentally rehearse your Connect story.	Think about what you might say to further amplify your belief with some additional belief statements.
Identify a different listening tip that you may be less familiar with than some others.	Mentally rehearse a story that a skeptic you know might tell to justify their view.
Remember, this is just practice. Use this as a learning experience.	Remember that you are not trying to win an Oscar.

Execute Role Play (4 min)

Ally Role Play Actions	Skeptic Role Play Actions
	1. Say a racially problematic viewpoint that this skeptic might say. Notes from step 1 should be helpful.
2. **Reflect:** Complete a Listening Tip, then get the skeptic to say more about their beliefs. For example: "That is an interesting point of view. Say a bit more about your belief."	
	3. Paraphrase something heard in conservative media. Do NOT tell an anecdote.
4. **Ask:** Make an inquiry focused on their personal experience. For example: "It's great that you are a good news consumer, but I am very curious about personal experience that further confirms your view."	
	5. Tell their personal anecdote that they think would be aligned with their viewpoint.
6. Listen empathetically to make the Skeptic feel truly heard.	*Tune in to how much they feel truly heard by the ally.*
7. Create a transition and bring up their own Connect story. For example: "That reminds me of a story…"	
8. **Segue:** "Let me tell you another story…"	

Debriefing the Role Play (4 minutes)

Ally Reflections	Skeptic Reflections
How did your Listening Tip work? How did hearing the skeptic's story feel?	How much did your partner make you feel heard when you told your story?
How did it feel to tell your Connect story?	How did it feel to play the role of the skeptic? What was difficult or easy about it?
What improvements would you like to make on your performance?	Any tips to help the ally sharpen their performance?

Switch Roles and Repeat

Appendix E: Practicing The RACE Method Through The *Expand* Step

Choose who is going play the role of the skeptic first.

Execute Role Play (6 min)

Ally Role Play Actions	Skeptic Role Play Actions
	1. Make a statement that is similar to one from step 1 of Boot Camp.
2. Take a brief pause to **Reflect** and implement a Listening Tip. Ask follow-up question to get skeptic to say more about beliefs.	
	3. Expand on beliefs by referring to an idea from a conservative media outlet. Do NOT tell an anecdote, stay with the belief.
4. **Ask** about past or recent experience related to their beliefs.	
	5. Tell a story that supports beliefs.
6. Listen empathetically enough to make the Skeptic feel truly heard.	*Tune in to how much they feel truly heard by the ally.*
7. Create a transition, then tell a **Connect** story. For example: "That reminds me of a story..."	
8. Create a **Segue** after letting the connection exist for a moment. Do NOT use the word "but" to introduce a second story. For example: "It's funny, another story is also coming to my mind..."	
9. Tell an **Expand** story that highlights unconscious bias and makes the point that racial bias still sometimes exists in our own hearts and minds.	*Listens empathetically.*
Optional: Ask if two things that seem the opposite of each other can both be true.	

Debriefing the Role Play (5 minutes)

Ally Reflections	Skeptic Reflections
What did you do to get in/stay in a listening mode? How well did it work? How did hearing the skeptic's story feel?	How much did your partner make you feel heard during your story?
How did it feel to tell stories? How did your experience of telling the different stories compare?	How did it feel to play the role of the skeptic? What was difficult or easy about it?
What improvements would you like to make on your performance?	Any tips to help the ally sharpen their performance?

Switch Roles and Repeat